Widow to Widow

Widow to Widow

Thoughtful, practical ideas for rebuilding your life: challenges, changes, decision-making & relationships...

GENEVIEVE DAVIS GINSBURG, M.S.

FISHER
BOOKS

To Paul, my son

Publishers: Bill Fisher
                   Howard Fisher
                   Helen V. Fisher
Editor: Bill Fisher
Managing Editor: Sarah Trotta
Cover design: Randy Schultz
Production: Deanie Wood

Published by
Fisher Books
4239 W. Ina Road, Suite 101
Tucson, AZ 85741
(520) 744-6110

Library of Congress Cataloging-in-Publication Data

Ginsburg, Genevieve Davis.
   [To live again]
   Widow to widow/Genevieve
Davis Ginsburg.
      p.   cm.
   Originally published: To live again:
Los Angeles: J.P. Tarcher, 1987.
   Includes index.
   ISBN 1-55561-153-2
   1. Widows—United States—Life
skills guides. I. Title.
HQ1058.5.U5G56   1997
305.48'9654—dc21   97-44910
                            CIP

                   Printed in USA
                   Printing 5 4 3

Notice: The information in this book is true and complete to the best of our knowledge. It is offered with no guarantees on the part of the author or Fisher Books. The author and publisher disclaim all liability in connection with use of this book. Fisher Books are available at special quantity discounts for educational use. Special books or book excerpts can also be created to fit specific needs. For details please write or telephone.

Contents

Acknowledgments

THE PAGES THAT FOLLOW CLEARLY SHOW my indebtedness to all the widows who have shared with me their pain, their tears, their laughter, and their struggle. There would be no book without them. I am especially grateful to all those who tarried a while to lend a hand to others. For without them WIDOWED TO WIDOWED SERVICES never could have happened.

My deep appreciation also to all the wonderful women in Tucson, young and less young, single and coupled, for all their affectionate pats on the back and friendships—what every widow needs on her way up. I feel lucky to be part of a community where women, even though they insist on calling it *networking,* really help each other.

Preface

SOME YEARS AGO MY HUSBAND DIED while playing tennis. A classic situation, and I, the classic widow, bravely modeled myself in the Jackie Kennedy image, coping in public and appearing to go on with my life. A marriage counselor by profession, I knew all the problems and had all the solutions. And as a member of a group practice, I had the added advantage of the professional and personal support of my colleagues. I had a career, education, economic security and good friends. I was lucky, everyone told me. They told me I was still young (in my mid-50s), attractive and handling "it" admirably. I would make it.

My terrible secret was that I was a terrible fraud. As soon as I left the office each day and got behind the wheel of my car, I burst into tears of anger and pent-up grief. I would stop at a supermarket for food I did not need and did not eat, warding off for as long as possible the homecoming that screamed the absence of the words and love that had for so long been the fabric of my daily life. I felt I couldn't make a decision and then in desperation finally made a poor one. I felt madly compelled to become an expert in finances, plumbing, electricity and eating out alone in restaurants. I couldn't read, remember what people said or not smile in public. I was worried that I would get the flu and die for lack of chicken soup. I fantasized about the boy who sat next to me in the first grade, the boy I dated in high school, and a half dozen others whose last names I couldn't recall. Saturday nights were worse than other nights. Maintaining a cool exterior over the seething, insecure, incompetent person that I felt myself to be was a continuous struggle. No one knew. No one except, I was to discover, another widow.

With another widow I could cry a tear and laugh at some of my daily tragedies; we could admit to our craziness and be mutually reassured. Unlike my coupled friends and professional colleagues, another widow did not tell me how well I was doing and how well I looked. Both were devastating conversational openers: I wasn't, and if I did, I shouldn't.

Of course I got on with it. The tears lessened, the craziness abated somewhat, and I got better at getting on with it. Now I really knew some of the problems and realized that I did not have all the solutions. Although still outwardly the model of a coping widow and inwardly mushy, I thought I ought to share my authentic expertise by starting a support group for widows.

Envisioning a typical group of eight or ten, I placed notices through the media for a meeting of widows interested in forming a self-help group. In spite of a downpour that day, 83 women arrived—women from different backgrounds and experiences but with a clear single need: to give to and receive from each other. What was to emerge from this first meeting was not the self-perpetuating group, wherein group members would stay to lead a new group and I would go on with my life and counseling practice, but a full-scale organization, wide in scope, for widowed people of all ages and both sexes.

Instead, it was my counseling practice that paled. The problems couples brought to marriage-counseling sessions sounded petty and picayune by comparison to those of the widowed. When those couples spoke of being "bored" and doing "something for myself" I felt like telling them to stop being spiritless crybabies, to work, endure and struggle; that the best was yet to come; and that a good marriage was 90 percent boredom and 91 percent "being there" for each other. This formula would have been seconded by thousands of widows who looked back at boredom with envy, but the words, of course, were hardly acceptable—or even helpful—to my paying clients.

My colleagues and friends shook their heads, mystified that I would find such a concentration of widows not only not depressing but also exhilarating, and a volunteer job more rewarding than one that paid 50 dollars an hour.

After a long sabbatical from which I have never officially returned, I changed my sign to read WIDOWED TO WIDOWED SERVICES and settled into directing the self-help organization as a full-time volunteer and a full-time learner. No job has given me greater pleasure, taught me more about courage, allowed me to observe such wisdom, or enriched me so with the warmth of humanity. I've been at it since 1977, and I still do not know all the problems and solutions that I thought I knew as a marriage counselor.

I never planned to write a How-I-Did-It or a How-to-Do-It book. My own enthusiasm was for mutual-help groups, and that's where I preferred to put my energy. One day, though, I began to notice the startling number of times new participants to the support group asked the same theoretical question, "Why didn't anyone ever tell me it would be like this?" And while the answer was often nothing more specific than "I know, I know," it was always magically reassuring.

That was the beginning of this book: to tell what widowhood is like by way of all the "I knows"—to lessen the sense of isolation each widow initially feels and to dispel the restrictive myths and burdensome rules about widowhood. In short, because only a small percentage of widows, and a smaller number of widowers, will ever join a support group—for such reasons as apprehension, the notion that strong people don't flinch, feeling apart and dread of the widow image—I wanted to encapsulate for the whole widowed network the essence of mutual help. This book is really a support group between covers.

The following pages are a combination of my thoughts and experiences and those of hundreds of widows—and widowers— who have passed through WIDOWED TO WIDOWED SERVICES in Tucson, Arizona, and of our struggles to grow from one-half a couple to a whole person. The quest is *wholeness*.

In the Company of Others

EACH YEAR MORE THAN A MILLION PEOPLE will join the 13.8-million widows and widowers in the United States. Yet each time it happens, it is a uniquely individual sorrow as though it never happened before.

In this book we are talking about widowhood as still another cycle in life. When we approached adolescence, adulthood, parenthood and other passages, we tackled those experiences with equally human variations and found we got through them better in the company of others. For me, adolescence became bearable after I read about Juliet and other suffering heroines; and motherhood sat more easily on my shoulders after talking to other mothers in the park while we pushed swings to and fro and seesaws up and down. So too has widowhood become a plausible continuation of life—with other hands on mine. It has happened before.

We are all different, yet we meet, touch, feel and need at so many similar places that we are connected. It is those connections that make up this book. What follows is what widows really talk about when they talk to each other or, as my grandmother would have said, what is really in their hearts. Dealing with the disposition of the old tweed jacket is not a suitable subject for discussion with a banker, an accountant or even one's children. But incredibly, that may be what is crucial and uppermost for a widow on a particular day because that is the stuff that grief is made of.

Just as people differ in the way they approached earlier life cycles, they will differ in the way they handle widowhood, and with consistent unpredictability. Although they made successful transitions in the past, they will not necessarily be prepared for this change. As you read the pages that follow, you will see that widowhood, at its worst and at its best, begins in a state of profound sadness. It can, remarkably, arc upward toward self-fulfillment—but is never straight, never constant, never perfect and certainly never easy. One doesn't forget or "get over" the past. Why should one? That would mean forgoing the times of love and laughter in the bargain. Exchanging that for a painless today is not a good enough trade-off. It would be like building a house from the attic up, with no foundation.

Along with many other suppositions, we are advised that grief has a set pattern. Social scientists have in recent years applied their analytical scalpels to the process of grief. They've concluded that yes, there is a course most of us follow in mourning. Influenced by Elisabeth Kübler-Ross' work on death and dying, they've developed what we glibly call the *stages of grieving*. Many of us had a book or pamphlets pressed into our hand by a minister, funeral director or, in my case, a bank trust officer, that spelled out these stages and told us what to expect. With some variations, the stages are described as follows:

   ❦ SHOCK AND DENIAL The period when death is recognized but not yet fully integrated into reality. The person appears calm, rational and emotionally contained on the outside and is automatically programmed from the inside.

   ❦ CONFUSION When the mind is overloaded with thoughts, demands and decisions, along with the emerging reality. This period is marked by forgetfulness, irrational thoughts and behavior, and indecisiveness.

   ❦ EMOTIONAL RELEASE Characterized by tears and sudden outbursts. The person worries about these emotional releases because she previously felt more in control, and outside observers may consider them excessive.

   ❦ ANGER One of the hallmarks of widowhood, the "unfair" time when blame is often misdirected, inwardly or outwardly, and sometimes denied entirely and manifested through different emotions more acceptable to the person.

   ❦ GUILT Self-recrimination and self-blame for events of the past, unfinished business. "If only" and "I should have" thoughts prevail.

   ❦ DEPRESSION AND ISOLATION A period of pervasive sadness, self-pity and no interest in the world and the people in it. Depression is often the onset of reality and change of lifestyle.

❦ RECOVERY   The last stage. Acceptance is finalized and the widowed person begins to function independently and to make a new life.

Further, we hear that people will usually "heal" within a year and, finally, that while remarriage is the cure of choice, recovery is also possible for those who keep busy and have a positive attitude. With that information, your grief package is signed, sealed and delivered, and you are supposed to be on your way.

The trouble is, this leaves many widows either believing they are not normal or else trying frantically to prove to themselves that they are, after all, just like everyone else. The notion of healing, normalcy and recovery suits our need for a fast, uniform cure, but not for truth. There is no cure for death, no recovery that renders us as we were before, and no correct way to survive the death of a beloved husband or wife. If you feel that way, be assured you are normal.

Because no one builds a new life single-handedly, the chapters that follow will also provide insights and answers for the friends, relatives and children who want to help in that effort but so often hesitate because they don't know how. I especially hope the children, who themselves have lost a parent and are confused about their future role and responsibilities, will find direction in these pages. Practitioners, who increasingly are dealing with the results of scattered family life and consequently are counseling more and more widows and widowers, will also find it useful to hear the voices of widowed persons rather than those of the heal-and-recovery theorists.

The text is divided into four sections, not because widowhood necessarily follows that course, but because it would be nice if it did. There is no one mold that we all fit into; this is the middle size.

"A Ton of Bricks" covers the shock of bereavement, the burst of emotions that follows, and the practical considerations many widows speak of during the early months.

"Rebuilding Your Life" speaks to the common experiences and problems that widows face when managing on their own once family and friends fade into the background.

"From Widowhood to Selfhood" addresses widows, regardless of "how long," and gives encouragement and advice for making what we know to be a variable accommodation to widowhood and a fickle transition to singlehood.

The fourth section, "Besides Which," provides important information for young widows, widowers and the children of the widowed.

There is also a resource section for widowhood and information on starting a support group in your community, plus a "Widow's Survival Checklist."

These sections are not intended to be sequential and, in fact, are not intended to sound the same each time they are read. Each day is new. Every reader brings his or her individual expertise to the subject, and as you know, an expert is someone who has done it—whatever it is—once. No one ever learned how to be a widow or widower without becoming an expert. From those who know then: this is what it's like to be widowed.

Part 1

A Ton of Bricks

THE BEREAVEMENT THAT FOLLOWS when someone close and beloved dies is the most profound of all emotional experiences. And because in an intimate relationship the lines of each individual have become blurred in fusion, the death of a spouse can be an aching separation. We mourn for the loss of ourselves. And equally true, the other person still lives on in us. Making the separation—the toughest assignment ever to come our way—is what we call *grieving*. While there have always been words to describe it and counsel on how to survive it, each one of us has to live it and sort out our own partings.

The pages in this section suggest what you might experience in going from the days of disbelief to accepting your separation as final. It also suggests that grieving is a process that you coax along by making friends with it. Those who get in trouble either expect too much of themselves too soon or believe in themselves too little. Be gentle with yourself, and don't ever underestimate your future. It may be some comfort to know that this period of grief—when the veil of numbness begins to lift and you first become aware of the dry springs in the flow of your life—is the most transitory period of widowhood. And that although it feels singularly desolate, it is shared by almost everyone who has lost something wonderful.

Widow

WIDOW. THE WORD ITSELF is so dreadful as to have no synonym, only a definition. It has a color: *black;* and associative words that immediately rise to the surface: *grief, tears, loneliness, poverty, panic, guilt* and *anger.* Experts on the subject of widowhood abound; everyone is out there giving advice, describing feelings, reciting the most recent stages of grieving like a rosary. They promise that time will heal, time will heal.

Only the widow feels ignorant. She is suddenly confused and incompetent—a total amateur. The advice and clichés she once offered others now defy her own belief. In no way did she fully anticipate or understand the depth of her feelings and the irrationality of her behavior. She cannot reconcile herself to what has happened.

That's how widows describe it, and only another widow knows what it feels like to become a widow. Her own grief seems more profound. Her own marriage—filled as it was with unspoken words, untranslatable looks and secret touches—was surely more special. Now, she is left with a lump of buried treasure sealed in its own tomb. Without the observer of who she was and who she is, she feels like nothing, a *zero.*

The first time I heard another widow verbalize those feelings I was shocked. How could this woman, so different from me in background, education, lifestyle—everything—be expressing my thoughts and feelings? You mean, her husband also thought she was adorable and sexy and was proud of her accomplishments? Well, yes and no. My relationship with my husband was unique. So was her relationship with her husband. What made us emotional sisters was our loss, our grief and our dismaying thoughts, common not only to the two of us but to others in our widowhood in general. Even my surprise at hearing another widow speak my very words is not unusual. There are, after all, over 13-million widows. However, we share about half a dozen basic human emotions, so that in our sorrow—our very individual and private sorrow—we feel and think and react in a set number of ways. Anger, envy, greed, love, hate, fear—any emotion, inscrutable problem, secret thought—another widow has lived it, thought it and survived it.

Most widows are comforted and reassured when they can connect with others in the same human struggle, but there are those who choose not to. They are the women who believe they should be able to cope on their own or that their individuality is diminished if they identify with other widows. For them, perhaps, the very word *widow* is loathsome, and the mental image the word conjures is humiliating. I recall a clear, frozen-in-time memory of the doctor telling me my husband was dead and thinking, "Oh my God, I'm a widow." That said it all.

First Hurdles

Widowhood is a club no one elects to join. Making peace with the new, unwelcome status, title and bleak image is one of the first stumbling blocks facing the new widow. As if it weren't bad enough to be confronted almost daily with papers and legal forms that read DECEASED after her husband's name, now she has to check off WIDOW as her marital status on form after form. Strange that she never paid particular attention to that category before.

Until it happens to us, the stereotypical widow is a vague "somebody else." There is also a tendency to equate widows with the elderly, mainly because so many of the elderly are widowed. A survey of people over the age of 70 shows that three-fourths of the population is female. The grim reality is that most women will outlive their husbands, and the sad truth is that they are of all ages. People are always surprised to find that the average widow is in her early 50s, and that her sample profile is Everyman's wife (average income, education, opinions and religious orientation); her resumé gives "homemaker" as her last job. She is Everywoman.

Grief Is an Equalizer

Although younger widows face some distinct problems—as you will read later—just as the elderly widow does, at the beginning the great equalizer of all widows is grief. An 80-year-old woman whose husband died in his sleep and a young woman whose husband was killed in a motorcycle accident are amazed to find they are undergoing the same process. "But you had so many years together," one is told; "You can start again," the other hears. However, they are both equally hurt, angry and confused. And it would be remiss not to add that men are no different from women in this regard and their sorrow is no less profound.

At an international conference of widowed-persons' organizations, variations of "I never realized what it would be like" were spoken in several languages. I heard a woman from Dublin say over tea, "I keep forgetting—that's the very worst of it. I think he's in the bathroom shaving, then when I look at the clock I think he'll be home soon. I know he's dead, I accept it. But I keep forgetting." That sounded familiar to the woman from France and the woman from Portugal, both of whom nodded understandingly. A young woman from Cameroon, quite a different culture (where, incidentally, widows have no property rights), was asked what her most pressing problem was. She answered promptly, "My in-laws." Everyone smiled knowingly.

The passage to widowhood is a rough one in any language. So much of it is a maze of unknowns. You need all the help you can get from friends and family, but at this particular time asking for help tends to stick in the throat. "Everyone thinks I'm doing so well," widows give as the explanation. They don't want to disappoint anyone.

There was never a widow who had nothing but kind thoughts, bore no malice or blame and believed she got a fair deal. But in many cases if she speaks her true thoughts aloud someone is liable to suggest that she "go

> *Most of us—to our own amazement—mobilize our inner resources and grow even stronger for having coped.*

for help." What it really means, though, is that the listener is distressed at hearing uncapped emotions and is passing the buck to another listener. Don't consider such a suggestion always to be a psychiatric diagnosis. For the most part, bereavement and grieving is a normal process requiring no medical or psychological intervention.

Handling the Death of a Spouse

How you handle the death of a spouse depends not only on your own response to crisis but also on individual personality patterns and your own hierarchy of needs. A chronically depressed wife will not turn into a merry widow unless her problem was more marital than chemical. A widow in frail health won't instantly be in the pink of health. But most of us—to our own amazement—mobilize our inner resources and grow even stronger for having coped.

If, because of a past experience, you feel professional support would be beneficial, by all means see a therapist, but don't look upon treatment as a sign that you are "crazy." Lynn Caine, in her book *Widow,* recalls: "Few of my actions had much to do with reality. They were freakish, inconsistent. Crazy. That's really what it was: craziness." Craziness is the normal nature of widowhood.

How one gets other kinds of help at this needy time is a true balancing feat. You need to share your grief but not your privacy; you need to take, but you don't want to give; and you want, you want, you want—what you can't have: You want *not* to be a widow.

You need to share your grief but not your privacy

The best help comes from friends, family or friendships with other widows. Other widows can be especially helpful because widows find friendships with other singles are an essential social lifeline. Mutual-help groups led by peers have a decided advantage over professionally led groups because they don't interject a you-need-help image. Support groups can shorten and soften the intensity of bereavement.

Eventually, you will restructure your life, but for now feel free to wear your grief in the best company you can manage. Know that you are strong and have untapped strength and an unrealized capacity for change; you are a survivor.

Numb and in Shock

MOST WIDOWS AGREE that during the first days or weeks they are in shock. They act like automatons, often efficiently, viewing their automatic functioning quite objectively, as though they were two different people. They have little recollection of events during this early period. This stage of shock and numbness is so common it is predictable. It may be Nature's cloak of protection, as some suggest, or one widow after another imitating what is currently socially acceptable. For us, Jacqueline Kennedy set an example for simple, stoic self-control that still serves as a model. And men have tearlessly braved it out for so long that most people squirm in discomfort when a man cries because it seems unnatural. Those of us who have gone through the death of a spouse recognize it at once for what it is: numbness and shock.

"I was so gloriously brave: I stood at the door of the church smiling and thanking people for coming as though it were a wedding reception. I wanted everyone to feel comfortable and no one to pity me," was how one widow described the way she greeted the many friends and congregation members who came to pay their respects to her husband, a well-known family doctor.

"All I could think of during the funeral was how pleased he would have been to see so many people and how he would have approved of all the details I had handled and decisions I had made. It was weeks before I realized the play was over and he was dead," another said sadly. Only three months earlier, her husband, a robust, seemingly healthy police sergeant, had suffered a sudden heart attack while shaving.

"People talked to me, but I have no idea who was there or what they said. Neighbors brought food; my freezer was filled with food, and to this day I couldn't tell you where it came from or who ate it," said still another widow—a high-school math teacher who prided herself on her logic and sharp recall.

One woman, a British war bride who spoke of herself as "totally dependent," was still unable to piece it all together: "A week after I buried my husband I went out and bought three rooms of maple furniture. I actually can't remember what I could have been thinking. I can't even remember what the salesman looked like. It's all a blank."

Participation Is Important

Those who say they were too stricken to function or too drugged on sleeping pills recall even less. They often feel cheated rather than spared. One woman, whose four daughters arranged all the funeral details and took turns staying with her for the following month, regretted her isolation. "I think if the girls hadn't been so good to me and I had my hands in it all along, I would have come out of the fog sooner." Most agree that while it is a blessing to have the active support of family and friends at this time, the widow needs to be a participant, not a spectator, at her husband's funeral. Not only family, but doctors as well—with tranquilizers and sleeping pills—want to spare her from the sight and business details of death.

Widows who dealt with the good-byes and funerals say they are grateful and proud they did, even though their strength was surprisingly temporary and fleeting. Surprising to them because the protective shield of numbness that kept them from absorbing more than they could handle was deceptively real at the time. "I don't know how I did it," widow after widow wonders.

When death is sudden, widows say they function as though programmed; with wifely continuity. The widow is still the wife acting according to what she perceives as her husband's desires, and the burial and funeral details unfold accordingly as he would have wanted. When death occurs after a long illness, the shock is not as pervasive. Often, final arrangements have already been discussed. Nevertheless, those widows describe having similar reactions. "I had rehearsed it all in my head so many times," one widow recalled, "that when the time came I was like a robot with absolutely no sensations.

Everyone thought I was magnificent."

Another told how she scrupulously followed her husband's request for no fuss and no funeral or memorial service: "It never entered my mind to do otherwise. I almost didn't exist as a thinking person. Months passed before I realized that I was doing myself a disservice. Finally the children and I held a memorial concert for his friends and fellow musicians, and we were all able to put him to rest."

Reality Sets In

Most people assume the worst is over with the funeral and the brief mourning period that follows. And because the widow has held up so bravely, they can go back to their own lives with an easy conscience. But once friends and family disperse, reality sets in. It is then that the widow's mental wires start to reconnect with the physical ones. Emotions are released as in a storm after the calm. Emotions and behavior, often as difficult to accept as is the loss itself—particularly with those who have up to now been showing an admirable façade—come pouring out uninvited.

> *No widow is prepared for the barrage of feelings within her.*

No widow is prepared for the barrage of feelings within her. "No longer in charge," "going crazy," "obsessed with his absence," and "filled with rage" are just some of the ways widows describe their inner turmoil at this time. And how are they supposed to know that their anxieties, panic, fear and anger ares emerging as "hateful thoughts" and "weird ideas"? The stages of grieving mention *emotional release,* but surely what I am going through is not normal, the widow thinks. And so she hugs her wicked self to her secret place like a child who has told his first lie.

Can you, the widow, believe that you are realizing and absorbing the fact that your husband is dead . . . and how your life is changing? Can you believe that your feelings are a healthy response to reality, that the numbness is lifting and the anesthesia is wearing off? Believe it. Talk to another widow. You are grieving. The time to deal with these gut-level feelings and frenetic brainwork is now, not later. When one widow checks out her fears and anxieties with another widow, she discovers she is not such a misfit after all.

This period is the widow's time of greatest need, but, alas, the time when you are least able to use your support system. This is mourning at its worst. While each of us has to know it personally, this is the time when you need reassurance and the ubiquitous shoulder to lean on. This is the time for honest disclosure with family and friends who pay no mind to hateful thoughts and can listen to months of "I don't know," "if only," and "I can remember when" without a sign of boredom.

Avoid all those who counsel you just to keep busy and not "think about it," those who change the subject should a tear slip past your guard, those who look right past your eyes, and especially those who greet you heartily with "You're looking well" followed by impersonal commentary on national affairs. What you need now is to have your loss acknowledged, your husband mourned, and your grief recognized. That's how others help you and how you help yourself.

> *What you need now is to have your loss acknowledged, your husband mourned, and your grief recognized. That's how others help you and how you help yourself.*

Dumb Things People Say

What friends, relatives
and those who care should know

MY GRANDSON, on arriving bleary-eyed at the time of his grandfather's sudden death, greeted me with "Well, I guess everyone's dead." During the next week I was to discover that this 3-year-old was one of the few people who could comfortably speak the word *dead*. If any of my many visitors, after offering the customary sympathy message and long look, accidentally uttered the word in my presence, fast talking quickly followed d-e-a-d silence. Phrases like "died laughing," "dying to go," "dead tired," "dead to the world," and "like death warmed over" would cause a roomful of people to stop— you guessed it—dead in their tracks. I was also to discover that if I mentioned my husband's name they would nod and shake their heads empathetically, but rarely did they prolong that bit of conversation. I liked my grandson's approach better. With him I could talk about Grandpa.

People are uncomfortable with death; death has been properly sanitized and professionalized so we can avoid the unpleasantness. Most of us got our first glimmer of the deception at the funeral home, where, sure enough, the place is decorated to resemble a private home. You might have seen the small calculator discreetly placed on the little Duncan-Phyfe lamp table, but otherwise you would never associate the surroundings with the itemized bill for services that followed.

Acknowledging the Loss

There are those who prefer to sweep the trappings of death and mourning under the table. But most widows want their loss *acknowledged,* not glossed over, and the name of their dead husband spoken, not avoided. They would like to tell callers not to bother if they are going to talk about the weather or how terribly funny their new poodle puppy is.

Widows wish folks could look them in the eye and leave off all the platitudes and poses.

And later on, when they meet, they wish friends and acquaintances wouldn't try so hard to avoid mentioning the subject. The omission is glaring. "Sorry if you're feeling uncomfortable," they would like to tell them, "it's worse for me. Don't stand there on one foot ready for flight, like a crane. He is dead, you can say it. It is not contagious. In fact, if you were to mention his name and some little memory of him, you would be giving me a gift."

Widows frequently speak about the ineptness and insensitivity people display in their presence. While admitting that they are unusually sensitive and impossibly difficult to be with at this time, widows wish folks could look them in the eye and leave off all the platitudes and poses.

They wish well-wishers wouldn't say "Please call me if you need any help" unless they are prepared to be called at 3:00 a.m., when you need them most.

They wish Trudy wouldn't offer the assistance of her handy husband to "fix anything, anytime" unless she is really sincere, because it might be 8:00 p.m. on a Saturday night when the light bulb goes out in the cathedral-ceiling fixture. If you call Nick, will Trudy be close behind? You bet.

Real friends do not say, "Call me if I can do anything;" rather they spell out what they can and will do and will check periodically to see if they are needed. The most unforgettable sympathy note I received was from an older widow who wrote, "I can cook a wicked stew, write thank-you notes in a good hand, sew neat hems and know how you feel. I'll phone you for my assignment."

Widows wish their well-intentioned friends wouldn't say, "Let me know when you feel like it" after the first perfunctory dinner invitation is declined. True, widows are impossible to please; they are offended when not invited and decline when they are. Every widow understands that conflict—why can't their friends?

Everyone Is Different

Some widows will take umbrage at last-minute invitations, while others prefer the informal—no decision required—warm invitation to "Come over. There's a nice roast in the oven, and we'd like to have an evening with you." Eight out of ten widows would say "yes" to that. Also, new widows do not mix well with couples with whom they previously shared subscription tickets, football games, bridge and after-church brunches if those friends insist on pretending that nothing has changed. Every widow knows their coupled friends feel guiltily grateful that they are still a couple and she feels guiltily envious that she is no longer part of a couple. She would like to reassure those friends that her envy is not specific and not to worry, and to ask them, "Please don't look down at your feet and say, 'You're looking great!'"

Invariably, "You're looking great" is the first sentence heard when the widow gets back into the mainstream. That looking-well greeting has come to be known as the "widow's opening gambit" and is heard constantly during the first two years. Admittedly, it leaps across the awkward social gap her presence creates, but as one widow put it, "How can I look so good when I feel so bad? And if I look so good, what am I doing wrong?"

Slightly different, but equally provoking, is, "I'm so proud of you. You're doing so well." For many widows, this innocent, reinforcing statement somehow implies rejection, not praise.

"They make it sound so easy. I'm not doing well. It's so hard. Can't they see?" one widow asked tearfully when this grievance was being discussed at her weekly widow's support-group meeting. She was reporting her unhappy experience of going back to her duplicate bridge club that week.

Another widow, whose husband had lost a three-year battle with cancer, agreed with her. "I feel as though I'm being complimented for having gotten over it," she said.

"They say it to avoid hearing anything unpleasant," explained a widow of longer standing. "It's for their own benefit, it makes them feel better."

"I feel tempted to reply, 'If you really knew, you'd give me an Academy Award,'" one young business executive said. "I wish I could tell them they are denying me my license to grieve openly. When I come back to work on a Monday morning after a long, lonely weekend, nothing ends a conversation faster than telling me how great I'm doing. One word out of my mouth and the tear ducts get activated, and one tear would destroy the act. If only they would say 'I know you're having a tough time,' we could cry together."

How Are You Doing? Awful!

"How are you doing?" is another one of those foolish questions. The answer to that is already obvious. Awful! One woman told how a friend called and asked not "how" but "what" she was doing, and it took a few minutes before she realized that her friend really cared to hear how she was living that hour of that evening of that day. As it turned out she was at that moment trying to eat her first TV dinner. Recounting that tragedy helped turn it into a comedy.

Not quite in the same class with "That was a stunning dress you wore to the funeral," but heard more frequently is, "You're so busy, you are never home." Widows wish people would go easy on that one. During the "running stage" widows find home easier to run from than to. One woman said her neighbor not only commented regularly on how busy she seemed, but also claimed to "envy" her social life. "It probably was meant as a compliment,

> *What we would like people to know is: Don't act as though nothing has changed; a squeeze of the hand and a square meeting of the eyes is better than a vacuous comment any time, any day.*

but I wanted to punch her in the nose. Instead, I offered to change places with her, and she hasn't spoken to me since."

The temptation to make a nasty reply isn't limited to that widow alone. A verbal punch in the nose makes some of us feel better—at least for the moment. In the early stage of widowhood words and phrases are heard with new ears. It takes very little to set the spring, the mechanism of which is anger. One usually law-abiding woman deliberately flattened a road sign on her street that read DEAD END. For her, the literal meaning of the term had changed overnight. Luckily, by the time she confessed what she had done, she could laugh at herself.

People have always said dumb things at times of distress. I shudder to think how many times—before I learned better—I ended a note of sympathy with "Please let me know if there is anything I can do." Widows, I suppose, could be more open and forthcoming with their own responses and feel less hurt and angry, but I'm not sure that words cover all the possibilities. What we would like people to know is: Don't act as though nothing has changed; a squeeze of the hand and a square meeting of the eyes is better than a vacuous comment any time, any day.

How Long Does It Take?

HOW LONG DOES IT TAKE? Undoubtedly, that's the question new widows ask most frequently. Every widow knows what it means. Will there ever be a day when I feel happy, when I no longer greet each morning with the fresh realization that he is dead, when I don't automatically turn to tell him something, when I no longer hear the roar of hollow silence as I come home to an empty house? When will I stop crying when someone says a kind word of sympathy or feel like crying because they don't? Will I ever stop feeling outside the world, an alien, alone?

The answer is "yes," in your own time and in your own way: gradually going forward, faltering, falling back, going on again—in any of the predicted or not-so-predicted sequences. In our society time circumscribes all events. There is a specified time allotted for getting born, beginning school, paying off the mortgage, healing a broken bone; at least you know it *will* happen. Here there is no time and no sure thing.

Some religious customs used to require the wearing of black for a full year—it's still observed in some places—not only to honor the dead but to signal the resumption of life when the year ended. The custom of wearing mourning clothes may be gone, but the time frame persists because we often hear people say, "It's been a year; she's not doing very well" or give good marks for "doing so well" in a shorter time. It would probably come as a surprise to those who knew me at the time, but my second year was worse than the first. The first year I was coping with a capital "C," perhaps to my own admiration; the second year I realized coping was not a temporary measure. This was *it*.

I often wish we could drop the whole vocabulary that has come into recent usage on death and dying that so glibly forecasts how we shall respond to the death of a spouse. The so-called *stages,* described here earlier, were never intended to become a mandatory blueprint for dealing with grief. They were observations of responses to personal loss. Using the medical model for grief—from shock to recovery—is a deception. Because we live in a quick-fix time, every illness must have a cure, and for every cure there must be an illness.

Implied is the promise that if you carefully go through the stages of grieving you will recover. The message is: You have the illness, we have the pill. If you have not fully recovered then you must have skipped a stage, become mired in a stage or denied a stage. It is *your* fault, *you* did something wrong. Guilty again! Widows have trouble enough with guilt; they do not need to be told they're in a messed-up stage to add to the problem.

> *Let us define the stages of grieving at the outset as feelings or emotions or a state of mind, and know that they come and go like the tide.*

How long does it take? is a silly question, because widowhood is not a disease, sickness or mental illness. It is a fact of life and there is no recovering. You learn to live with it, cope with it and survive it. You will get pretty good at it as time goes by. The tears will abate, the anger soften and the future will be brighter than today. But you will not be cured, not even if you remarry.

So let us define the stages of grieving at the outset as feelings or emotions or a state of mind, and know that they come and go like the tide. With the possible exception of the initial shock and numbness that follows a deep loss, the so-called *stages of grieving* can and do return unpredictably with pristine sharpness any time, any day, any year—and that is no sin.

When recovery is the touted outcome—the expected outcome—the widow feels inadequate and abnormal if she has not "gotten over it" in her allotted time. She can be heard to apologize, "There is something wrong with me." It has been three months, six months, two years—whatever—she is still crying, and she can't get over it. She has failed the time test. She is still full of tears and anger, she says. She still feels jealous and sad when she sees couples holding hands, still feels confused and rudderless, still cannot let a day go by without thinking of his dying and what she might have done, could have done, should have done. "I know I should be over it by now," she sobs.

"Six-Month Syndrome"

Worse, another widow may suffer what she believes is a setback after having steadily moved onward and accepted her reality: "I was doing so well, everyone was so proud of me, and for no good reason I've suddenly started going backward." Tears at the drop of a hat, physical symptoms that prove to be groundless, a hand tremor that began with the first formidable document and grows more embarrassing each day, and finally, feeling hopeless and missing him more than ever. We call this

> *Widowhood is dotted with sudden realizations . . . that account for the many emotional highs and lows.*

the *six-month syndrome* because that seems to be when progress most often founders. It is also the time when family and friends worry and express concern. "It's been six months and my mother is doing worse; she's crying more now. What shall I do?" Mother is doing what her daughter did after taking her first step a long time ago: She fell down.

The six-month syndrome may occur at any time (I experienced mine after two years). Widowhood is dotted with sudden realizations—some very scary—that account for the many emotional highs and lows. As shock and numbness fade, the widow becomes more clear-headed. She begins to reconstruct her identity and becomes increasingly aware of how many changes she will have to accept and how many crises she will face single-handedly. With a sudden jolt, she thinks perhaps she will never become used to being alone at night, or maybe that pain under the left rib is the beginning of cancer. Or as one woman recalled, "I couldn't pull the damn zipper up the back of my dress and that triggered one of my lowest periods. I cried for two days. It really hit me that I was alone and I'd have to lose 50 pounds or wear a Hawaiian muumuu for the rest of my life." Later, more mundane reminders rise to bait the new widow—little things, like having no escort for the annual Heart Fund Ball, and hundreds of other first-time realizations that run the gamut from struggling to open the mayonnaise jar to traveling alone.

If she speaks with friends about the emptiness she is experiencing during these low periods, she will hear, "You're feeling sorry for yourself." Her family is the audience for bright thoughts, not black ones. The widow herself becomes the most distressed if she suspects she may indeed be feeling sorry for herself. For no convincing reason, self-pity is judged to be the worst of all possible sins.

On the other hand, self-pity is actually more desirable than other people's pity and feels pretty good when you are just plain tired of coping. Feeling sorry for yourself is like putting your emotional feet up—resting between coping bouts and catching a second wind. Overdone, of course, it can become a bore for everyone.

Once you stop equating good days and bad days with success and failure and grading yourself on performance, your energy is freed for better use than self-reproach. Reassure your family and friends—and your doctor—that sometimes neither you nor they can tell what stage you're in. Today, it might be the stage called *regression* or be all of the stages simultaneously.

Anger is a troubling emotion for some people to admit into their consciousness. Depression comes in many disguises, and confusion may become so pervasive that it feels natural. You've heard people say, "She only hears what she wants to hear". Well, it's the same with emotions. The true value in taking a look at our emotional reactions to grief is not so we will identify and label ourselves, but that we give ourselves the right to feel the way we are feeling. "You mean it's OK to

Grieving is a process rather than a series of uphill steps, and gains are most often realized in retrospect.

feel sorry for myself? Angry? Useless? It's been eight months, I thought I was supposed to be over that." You'll always have a little left over for another time.

Grieving is a process rather than a series of uphill steps, and gains are most often realized in retrospect. One day you will realize that a whole day has passed without thinking about him. You actually enjoyed yourself for an entire weekend, that this Christmas was better than the last, that the little knot of envy has worked its way free, and that the good days far outnumber the sad ones. How long did it take? Six months? A year? Two years and three months? Only you can say. But it does happen, in your own time and in your own way.

> *One day you will realize that a whole day has passed without thinking about him.*

Making a
Full Day of It

ONCE THE MOST IMMEDIATE tasks are attended to, widowhood does not take up too many hours of the day. Until now your time centered around another person with whom and for whom the day turned. Now it's all yours and there is far too much of it. That's why you need a plan, made in advance, to carry you along until you have broken from the old routines and are able to settle into new ones.

Breakfast alone may loom like a black hole. The strong desire to roll over and never get up is considerably abated when you replace your old automatic program with another. Be it walking a mile, picking up a newspaper before breakfast, or fixing a tray before a sunny window, have your plan in mind so you rise and go to it without thinking. Morning becomes livable when you do something cheering and healthy for yourself.

As for the rest of the day—without meals to prepare, the old errands and social engagements—many women, so-called *housewives* who do not have a regular job to return to, say they "run out of the house." They spend time walking aimlessly through shopping malls and come home only to watch television and get ready for another day like the one before. Dreary, isn't it? However, with advance planning, that same time-filler can become a shopping excursion, a trip to the museum, a lunch or dinner diversion, and a social meeting. Planning makes for a not-so-dreary day because you are *making it happen* rather than passively *waiting for something to happen*. Your plan need only consist of a few objectives, even such mundane chores as doing laundry, grocery shopping, catching up on correspondence or going to the bank—but built around a schedule, your day will seem more purposeful. Checking off accomplishments as you go gives you an opportunity to pat yourself on the back at a time when you can use every pat on the back you can get.

Evening Commitments

Women who work outside the home feel lucky to have their daytimes occupied, but find their evenings studded with sameness. Because it is so much easier to go home and wait for tomorrow, they avoid planning for new friends and activities; they, too, wait for it to happen. But it doesn't. Even more than the homemaker-widow, working women need regular evening and weekend commitments.

Activities after dark, depending on your particular geography, climate and mobility, may necessarily be restricted to asking someone over for dinner or spending the time in your own good company. This is when you write in your journal, read those library books, straighten your files, bring the photo album up to date and watch television *selectively*. Too much television is another one of those passive ("I'm not in charge") activities. Later on you will find more to do and more people to do it with.

Planning makes for a not-so-dreary day because you are making it happen rather than passively waiting for something to happen.

Weekends—Planning Is Key

Weekends are another matter. They seem designed to bring out the blues and the tears. One woman, who had been married and had not dated for 33 years, said she had such a terrible sense of failure every Saturday night because she could hear her mother nonchalantly asking whether or not she had a date. You never know what is going to surface, so it is mandatory that you preplan and not leave yourself with days when it seems that everyone but you has someplace to go. Spend some time on the phone calling friends, especially other widows. Arrange for at least one weekend activity. If you regularly go to church on Sunday, for example, plan to have company for the going and coming or a light meal afterward.

When there are children at home, younger widows too often try to be mother and father, leaving no time for themselves. When

Make Time for Activities

Widows, in listing those activities they found most helpful, suggest the following:

- Make a weekly trip to the library for such light reading as mysteries, biographies and inspirational books on widowhood.

- Check the newspapers daily for events and activities open to the public—art, music and politics. The subject is not as important as being out with people and exposing yourself to something new and possibly challenging.

- Collect investment information and attend investment seminars— without making a promise or commitment.

- Enroll in an exercise class suited to your physical capabilities and not those of a 16-year-old ballerina. Yoga is good and especially friendly.

- Set a regular time each week for bookkeeping and business-related errands so you are never overly occupied with the job or remiss.

- Start investigating and collecting information about classes, volunteer jobs, hobbies and training. Make no choices if you are still feeling confused and preoccupied. If you are a homemaker-widow, gather information about employment opportunities. Don't commit yourself to start work or return to work until you're ready.

- Join a weekly widows-support group.

- Get out and mingle with people and do it with a purpose. If you go to the park, feed the squirrels; or if you go shopping, have a specific purchase in mind.

- Make an appointment to have lunch or dinner with a friend at least once a week—more often if you are a working woman who has to maintain a façade most of the time and needs to let her hair down.

- Avoid committing yourself to any program that involves concentration or taking care of sick people unless you are sure you can handle it. You may be still too distracted to keep your mind clear and still too vulnerable to handle illness and death. Choose upbeat, short-term, interesting projects at the beginning because with these you are less likely to withdraw and feel a failure.

- Avoid taking on babysitting your grandchildren if it means you will be alone with them for long stretches. Visit but be free to leave when it feels right.

- Tape this sign to your bathroom mirror where you can't fail to see it every night:

DO NOT GO TO SLEEP WITHOUT A PLAN IN YOUR HEAD FOR THE DAY AHEAD.

adolescent children are involved, the reverse can happen. Believing that they have "a life of their own," mother and children may pass each other on the way out the door. A good solution in both situations is a weekly family meeting—an inviolate time—when the family members report in, discuss problems, clarify individual rights and make plans for the week ahead.

Working widows have to resist the temptation to hole up and wait for the workweek to begin, or to depend on coupled friends to call. If you have no single friends, join some kind of organized activity, preferably something physical such as health-club workouts, classes at the YMCA or YWCA, swimming lessons, or a similar program that will release endorphins—those juices secreted in the brain that energize. Sign up! I joined a hiking club because neither I nor my husband had been hikers before and there were no associative memories. On my first hike, a sizable number of people had to "talk" me to the top; I didn't think I would survive that trip. But that Sunday night I slept right through until Monday morning without once reaching out to the other side of the bed, and I knew I was onto something important.

Perhaps it is all a trick—a mental sleight of hand—but you are working on one of the toughest do-it-yourself jobs you've ever had to do. There will be days when you go on strike, have a temper tantrum and want to do absolutely nothing. Allow yourself a small rebellion now and then. Again, know that *you* are the leader in charge of the rebellion—not the victim—and then get up and give it another go.

Anger

WIDOWS ARE ANGRY. That's a fact. Some admit it, some deny it—and some don't even know it. They differ only in where and how they *focus* that anger.

Angriest of all is the widow who claims *not* to be angry. Smiling and tight-lipped, she insists that anger never solves anything. If you are such a person, one who has had a life of emotional containment and has always turned your anger on yourself rather than risk the rejection of another, you will undoubtedly approach widowhood the same way. But unvented wrath has to go someplace. No matter how tightly the cap is closed, your internalized anger will surely come out via one outlet or another: guilt, depression, self-recrimination, sugar-coated bitterness.

Take your pick. Justifiable or not, in widowhood you have much to be angry about. There's no really satisfactory way of resolving that anger if you keep taking it out on yourself. In one brief moment you have lost your place in your personal history, your life role, your daily status and the echo of who you are. Do you really feel no resentment, no hurt, no unbidden envy? Look again, for you may have misplaced one of your basic rights.

A Close Second to Anger—Hurt

A close second to the angerless widow is the *hurt* widow. Not able to indulge in a straightforward confrontation with God, the Fates or her dead husband, stand-ins take the blame. Is that you? At two o'clock in the morning are you writing letters in the air to the brother-in-law who hasn't surfaced since the funeral six months ago and the friend who feels so bad she can't bear to call? Your peers would advise you to write the letter in ink and *then* decide whether to mail or destroy it. With that choice you are no longer the victim, you are the navigator. Either way the action is cathartic: You have put words to your feelings and brought them outside. Whatever your hurt, don't keep it inside.

Anger at Doctors and Nurses

The same applies to anger directed toward doctors and nurses—a prime target for many widows. Most of the hostility directed against the medical profession by widows is justified not necessarily for malpractice, but for maladroitness. Doctors are better at dealing with life than with death. With present medical procedures calling for so many specialists, the entire process seems impersonal, as if no one cares. A sleeping pill is not the answer for the new widow. It will never replace 30 minutes of time and sympathy, but too often that is all the helping hand holds out these days. "This will help you sleep tonight." Unasked and unanswered questions remain in the mind. Over and over we hear:

"Why did he operate? Lou could have lived with his angina."

"He sent a bill promptly enough, but he never had time to return my calls."

"She was our doctor for so many years, but when my husband died she never called me. I felt so hurt, and I've never gone back to her."

"Why did he die? The doctor never explained it to me. He sent his assistant in because he couldn't face me. And try getting him on the phone . . ."

"The hospital didn't call me. I wasn't there when he died. I can't stop thinking about him being alone. Why didn't they call me?"

Agonizing over the immovable facts traps you in a whirlpool of misspent anger. Again, other widows will tell you to act. Make that call, ask those questions and write that letter. If the letter involves a question of money, by all means send it. Usually doctors have little to do with their billing and are amenable to justifiable adjustments as well as to the explanations you may not have heard under stress. You will usually get results. Act!

Listening versus Telling

Then there's the ancient-mariner widow, one who is consumed with fury and goes around repeating her story endlessly. If you ever hear yourself becoming tiresome and boring, it's time to be quiet and start listening to others. I recall one woman who never ceased blaming her son for persuading his father to undergo the surgery from which he never recovered. The son, a doctor himself, had agreed with the attending physician that surgery was necessary; the widow could forgive neither for that decision. Her bill of particulars and anger did not diminish no matter how often she vented her anger. She would not let go of it. Incredibly, one day another woman joined the support group she was attending and told a story so similar that no one could quite believe the coincidence. The first widow sat there listening, silent for the first time.

> *If you ever hear yourself becoming tiresome and boring, it's time to be quiet and start listening to others.*

Three weeks later, in a quiet patient voice, she addressed the new group member. "I used to feel the same way," she said, "but what good will come of losing your son as well as your husband? Last weekend I talked to my son"—exactly what everyone in the support group had been suggesting she do all along—"and I didn't blame him, but I said that I wished every day that we had not permitted the operation. My son said he felt the same way, and that although he knew his father's only chance required surgery he still couldn't forgive himself. I never realized he carried that around. He and I have never before been so close." She put her arms around the other woman and added, "You need a son more than you need someone to blame." In behavioral psychology that's called a *negative model,* and believe me, there is always one around.

More often, though, when it comes to blame, widows reproach themselves rather than others. In their omnipotence, deep down they believe they should have been able to foresee and forestall. They castigate themselves for the darndest things: "He worked too hard (for me)," "I should have made him go to the doctor," "I should have known . . ." and on and on, ad infinitum. I shoulda, I coulda. Mea culpa, trying to rearrange the pieces for a better picture.

Take Anger for What It Is

Widows looking for a logical answer ask "How can I be angry with God?" and "How can I be angry with my husband for dying?" They choose instead to feel guilty, hurt, deserted or zoom in with a vengeance on a real or imagined culprit. In the short run it may be more logical to fight with the gas-station attendant. But in the long run it is more productive to recognize anger for *what* it is and finally, *where* it is.

The *what* comes first. Healthier is the widow who can say she is as mad as hell and wants to kick the scales of justice to kingdom come. She hates the sight of sweet old couples walking hand in hand. As though bewitched, she finds herself focusing on how many utterly useless men are alive and well. She wants to lash out at people who invite her to a party, do not invite her to a party, tell her how well she looks, and especially, at those whose offer to help is as far away as the look in their eyes. She is mad, she is irrational and she knows it. What's more, although she has plenty of company, she is always surprised to find that other widows have equally hateful reactions and envious thoughts and that she is *not* uniquely evil.

I recall a woman in a support group who related how troubled she was by her response to telephone callers who, unaware that her husband, a big club member, had died, were still phoning about club business. A rather mild, shy woman, she at first politely explained the situation. As the calls continued, her words grew meaner and more shrill, until one day she told a caller the name of the cemetery and suggested how he might reach him. She was shocked at her own behavior and looked helplessly to the other widows.

Instead of the lecture she expected, she heard:

"I tell them to drop dead and hang up. I never talked to people that way in my life. Don't feel bad."

"Say, 'I'm sorry, that party is deceased.' That makes them feel awful."

" 'He died. I am his widow.' Just say that very quietly with a tear in your voice. That really gets 'em."

The last word for handling the problem—short-term, but satisfying—was: "Honey, tell them, 'He's not here now, and I couldn't tell you when he'll be back.' You'll still be angry, but you'll laugh instead of cry when you hang up the phone."

No one suggested she continue couching her hostility with polite standard clichés, because everyone understood how intertwined were her hurt and wrath. Wanting to strike back at any living person is understandable and, believe me, forgivable. The supermarket cashier who intones "Good day," the mechanic who offers to explain it to your husband, and all manner of people who are acting as though the world has not changed are insufferable to the person whose world has just collapsed. One woman, who was stopped for running a red light, screamed at the policeman, "How would you like your wife to get a ticket when her husband just died?"

> *No matter how often I read and heard that anger is a stage of grief, I was sure that would never apply to me.*

Anger at Your Spouse

Don't believe you have a corner on hostility. You will become socialized eventually and feel human again. The *where* is more convoluted. You are angry with *him,* but how can you denounce a dead husband so greatly loved and sorely missed? Recently a woman told me sharply, "I'll come to this widows' group every week, but no one will ever convince me that I'm angry with my husband for dying. He wanted to live." I knew just how she felt.

No matter how often I read and heard that anger is a stage of grief, I was sure that would never apply to me. But I can still remember the first time I was directly angry with my husband because it was so unexpected. It was six months after any of the 43

Anger is attached to grieving. Don't bury it in "only good and positive" thoughts.

assorted and miscellaneous keys in his top bureau drawer failed to fit any of the assorted and miscellaneous locks I tried. Like a compulsive nut, I couldn't pass a keyhole without doing a quick assessment. One day, in a flash of inspiration, I decided to try his former office building, and one of those errant keys got stuck in a mismatched lock to which I no longer had any claim. I tugged and tugged, someone came out to investigate the noise, and I muttered something about a mistake. The door closed, and suddenly furious I threw the keys up in the air leaving them scattered all over the fourth floor, my head screaming, Damn it, Martin, why didn't you label these keys? Roughly translated it comes out, *You had no right to leave me in this mess.* Suddenly, and for the first time, my rights were being violated, not his.

Since then I've heard hundreds of outbursts of anger:

"He could have stopped smoking, and I blame him for that."

"It's not fair! Dammit, just as we were beginning to have time for each other. He could have taken it easy."

"He took care of everything. He left me a blithering idiot."

"He always drove at night. Now I'm scared."

"I never wanted to buy this house; it was his idea."

And always, "Why did he leave me?"

To gain your anger-rights is no simple matter; there's no foolproof recipe. You may not have words to clarify your emotions, but you can recognize anger when it rises to the top. Anger is attached to grieving. Don't bury it in "only good and positive" thoughts. You know the ultimate outcome for martyrs. Don't let yourself become one. Failing words, try kicking the garbage pail around the block to get it out of your system. At this difficult stage in your life, you may forgive yourself unladylike behavior or a bit of ranting, accusing and illogical thinking. As one widow announced, "We are entitled."

At this difficult stage in your life, you may forgive yourself unladylike behavior or a bit of ranting, accusing and illogical thinking.

Guilt

GUILT is surely an early-born characteristic of widowhood. The widow feels guilty about being alive, about what she might have done, if not to change the outcome, then at least to have mitigated a detail or event. There is always something that, given another opportunity, could have been done differently and—maybe—with different results. But that's only Phase One guilt. As she goes through grieving and begins to get on with her life, the widow erects roadblocks of guilt on every side for new and other reasons.

She still feels guilty about being alive, feels ill at ease about spending his money, and ignores what may be his wishes. In general, managing some kind of transition that is leaving him behind is Phase Two guilt. Finally, Phase Three guilt occurs when, moving along, finding satisfaction in her ability to cope, and taking some pride in surmounting unfair and uneven odds, the widow takes on a kind of "Look, No Hands" guilt that is tinged with uneasiness as well as pride.

You might deduce from this that you are destined—sad or happy—to live with guilt forever. Wrong! You may choose to forgo it entirely, right from the beginning. Guilt is not a pure, basic human feeling such as anger, happiness, sorrow or fear. Guilt is a ruse, a cover-up, an instead-of mechanism, and we invoke it voluntarily. Guilt is the greatest little handy-dandy avoidance tool ever invented. Turn guilt over and you will find it made of fear and/or anger, but who wants to take a peek?

> *Guilt is the greatest little handy-dandy avoidance tool ever invented.*

More often than not we leave one little opening for blame. Guilty by self-decree; somehow, our womanly intuition and our omnipotent antennae were faulty, or we did wrong. Right at the beginning, as the family caretaker, the temperature taker, the dispenser of aspirin and chicken soup, women hold themselves responsible for their husband's health. In the case of a sudden, fatal heart attack the widow thinks, "I should have made him go to the doctor." In the case of a fatal automobile accident, "If only I had delayed him two minutes." And once I heard a woman blame herself for not having acted on her premonition that her husband who was boarding a flight for a business trip would be killed. The plane crashed, more than 100 people were killed, her husband among them, and she blamed herself. Wouldn't you say that was self-inflicted?

There is guilt over feeling relieved that the torture of a long, terminal illness is over. "Thank God he doesn't have to suffer anymore" also means "and I'm free of that burden." There is guilt when a wife can no longer possibly take care of her terminally ill husband at home. "He didn't want to die in the hospital; I let him down." There is guilt when suicide is the fatal outcome. Superwomen are guilty, never angry.

> *If you are thinking of giving or lending money to one of your children to start a business or buy a house (the two most common reasons), hold off. Default and hard feelings may be the repayment.*

Money and Guilt

Money is a big guilt producer. More particularly, insurance money. Reason says that life insurance was purchased for the very situation in which the widow finds herself. Guilt says, "He had to die for me to have this money, and it is not really right for me to keep it for myself." Women over 50 have limited access to jobs and group medical-insurance plans. When they, as well as others who have no prospect for adding to their capital, are fortunate enough to have a cushion to fall back on, they should hold on to that money with a bulldog grip. Usually that capital is invested for the income that may be realized, but very often the widow feels obliged to make some distribution to assuage her guilt. If you are thinking of giving or lending that money to one of your children to start a business or buy a house (the two most common reasons), hold off. Default and hard feelings may be the repayment.

The situation is often most difficult for the widow of an indulgent husband when she now has to be the bad guy. "Poor kid," one woman recounted to her support group, "he's never been as successful as his brother, so I lent him the money to go to radio-broadcasting school. He wanted to be a disc jockey, but he never got a job. It was two-thousand dollars down the drain. His father always worried about him. How could I refuse? Now he needs me to cosign an automobile loan. I don't have much, but I can't say no."

"Practice!" was the unanimous advice of her support group.

The widows were equally adamant with the woman who, having just returned from a visit with her lawyer-daughter, sobbed, "You're not going to believe this, but Jenny is hurt because I gave her sister and brother-in-law the down payment for their house. Jenny has a good job, she's not married. My other daughter needed help, but Jenny feels that she has just as much right to her Dad's money and I wasn't fair. I feel so guilty."

The verdict of her peers was, "It is your money, not Dad's."

> *When children of any age become fatherless, the widow tries to split herself down the middle to make up for the loss. You can't.*

Guilt, Money and Good Judgment

Most children do not begrudge their mother her inheritance. Not having the worry of financial responsibility is a greater gain for them. More often it is that unrelenting combination of mother and her guilt that muddies the water with her need to be evenhanded and self-effacing. One woman invited her two married children and their families on a Christmas trip to Hawaii soon after her husband's death. "I would have felt so guilty using that insurance money on myself.

Now I wish I had that money; I could use it."

A similar story was told by a woman who worked as a waitress and whose husband had died of a heart attack at age 46, leaving her with two daughters, 16 and 18. Luckily, he had both life insurance and home-mortgage insurance. Left with a free-and-clear mortgage, $50,000 in cash, and no experience in money management, this widow thought her first priority was her daughters' happiness. She walked into a department store and with the help of a willing salesman bought her daughters new furniture and a wall of stereo equipment—all in one swift deal. A year later she arranged a lavish wedding for the older girl. "It cost more than $10,000," she said, "but we did Don proud." Although miserable at math, she earned an A+ in guilt. Not you, I hope.

Younger widows with children have a battle resolving their conflict between guilt and good judgment. They say it's almost impossible at the beginning not to feel theirs is a two-parent responsibility. The question of "What would he have done?" often influences their thinking and is factored into decisions and problem-solving for a long time.

When adolescent children are concerned, mothers walk a tightrope between discipline and guilt, hesitating to exercise authority. Frequently adolescents will not grieve openly. Mothers—interpreting the children's silence as their failing—add to their own sense of guilt by avoiding the subject of father and his death.

Guilt is no help. Discuss it and keep the lines open, even if it seems you are sometimes talking to yourself, because if the subject appears unapproachable to you, it will continue to be so for the children as well. When children of any age become fatherless (see the chapter on Young Widows), the widow tries to split herself down the middle to make up for the loss. You can't. You can, however, always ask yourself whether you are acting out of guilt or reason. With time, under careful self-examination, you will give yourself a straight answer.

Guilt about Being Alive

A widow who feels guilty about being alive, enjoying herself, and leading a normal life is filling her head with other people's thoughts; that is, what she thinks other people are thinking. Her family will disown her if she goes on a trek in Nepal; the ladies in her church guild will be shocked if she wears her red dress; how can she be seen in public with another man? All of us experience a complex assortment of feelings about outliving our husbands. Most of us choose to go on living, and with that choice, joy and pleasure do eventually catch up to us once again. Understandably, there is often sadness that those pleasures are no longer shared. But, in fact, life cannot be shared with a dead husband.

You are alive, and you are entitled to make the best of it. Guilt is not the only route toward that goal. You can get there directly with no detours. However, the cost may be risking displeasure, disagreement and disapproval. You may have to acknowledge your own anger, cowardliness and irresolution and take the plunge to meet the person in you who has been waiting patiently, like a frightfully attractive genie. Once you understand how you can delude and pummel yourself with guilt, don't start feeling guilty about feeling guilty. Saying good riddance to guilt is Phase Four guilt, a lifelong process.

Who knows, you may end up liking yourself better. Harder? Riskier? Yes, but more rewarding and certainly less punishing.

You are alive, and you are entitled to make the best of it.

Decisions, Decisions

THERE OUGHT TO BE a coat of arms for widows: a crest showing a plaintively outstretched hand with the motto ON THE OTHER HAND written below (in Latin, of course). It's every widow's insignia.

Indecisiveness is a hallmark of widowhood. It's supposed to be one of the early stages, but, believe me, it can be long-term. New widows will identify one of their worst problems as not being able to make a decision. "Is there something wrong with me?" they ask. "I vacillate so much the house shakes."

Ambivalence is not a sign of mental deterioration, nor is it an unspeakable social disease. It is perfectly normal to feel insecure about suddenly being in charge after years of team-playing. When there are two players, the blame or credit gets diffused. You said (or perhaps just thought) it was his fault, and he said (or thought) it was yours; in times of triumph, you both took credit. Now it's *all* yours, and at a time when you still feel obliged to be of two minds: yours and his.

Acting from his advice and doing what he would have wanted gives many a widow a sense of security and confidence to deal with the funeral and other tasks initially. She is more likely to move with purpose and certainty one week after her husband's death than three months later. There is a familiar scenario to act out at the beginning—we take our behavioral cues from the widows we've observed. But no one is fully prepared for the utter confusion and panic that creeps in along with reality.

Like frosting on a cardboard cake, the widow is outwardly fine but inwardly phony. And her great fear is that she will be found out. No one—not even the electric company—must know how ignorant she is or how many mistakes she has made. As she goes on dealing with bills, endless paperwork, people and her own emotions, she really is not in prime condition for deciding even such simple matters as whether she wants bacon-and-tomato-on-wheat or chicken-salad-on-rye for lunch, let alone important decisions. Consequently she is shaky.

Women will wonder why they have suddenly become so inefficient and why they vacillate so much. "I used to take care of all the accounts," one widow said, "but yesterday at the bank I couldn't even decide on pink or yellow checks. I was so embarrassed I asked for white."

In contrast is the woman who was completely dependent on her husband and deferred to his word more often than not. Her dubiousness is not new. She looks up toward heaven for instruction and feels uneasy and uncertain about making a unilateral decision. One widow took two years to replace the badly worn carpeting in her house because she had never shopped for any major purchase alone. The day after it was installed she reported, "Green, I chose green. Arthur hated green, but it really does fit in perfectly and, you know, I like being right."

During the first year after my husband died I can recall being immobilized by indecision when it came to financial matters or having relatively minor home repairs made. I had three stockbrokers—a consultant, my cousin and my son, the tax lawyer. And when I had a ceiling fan installed, I got bids from four electricians. Always so sure of myself before, that year I was tentative and avoided major decisions through procrastination. It was difficult enough choosing between a black skirt or black slacks when I dressed in the morning.

A widow is more likely to move with purpose and certainty one week after her husband's death than three months later.

And I considered myself a pro. One of my past jobs had been counseling mental-health patients after release from the state hospital to adjust to independent living. On yellow legal pads, the patients and I listed the pros and cons, advantages and disadvantages, and thus determined the consequences of any action or inaction. Easy enough for a schizophrenic, but they didn't make yellow pads big enough for this widow. What I did was immobilize myself with overkill and overthink. If two out of three stockbrokers advised selling a particular stock, I would wonder what my husband knew that they didn't for him to have bought the stock in the first place. (He probably told me at the time, but who paid notice then?) I was trying to make a decision with three minds (broker, mine and his) and two hands, which certainly didn't help to make matters any better. When the dishwasher and washing machine broke down in rapid succession shortly after the funeral, I compiled such an exhaustive list of comparative features and prices that, based on my notes, Einstein himself could not have advised me how best to solve my problem.

I drove myself crazy over Martin's pistol collection: I wanted them out of the house, but he had loved those guns. I ought to learn to shoot now that I lived alone, I thought, but the nice police officer I called for advice said, "Forget it." The gun dealer would cheat me, I thought, maybe I should just give them away to one of his good friends. But, no, I needed the money, no, I could manage. I would be sorry if I sold them, I would be relieved. Had I had an ounce of objectivity working for me I could have left the guns as they had lain for the past ten years, unassembled, unused, safely out of sight and forgotten.

Just Do It!

Fortunately for me, about that time my 21-year-old niece came to visit me. She had just graduated from college and was trying to decide what to do with the rest of her life. She stayed for three months and took on my rehabilitation. Every time I'd begin one of my "I don't know whether I should . . ." sentences, Amy would say, "Do it. Just do it." And that is how I made some successful stock decisions (I bought AT&T stock), had the house painted white, and went on a vacation to Mexico. Ever since, my favorite line of instruction for myself and all indecisive widows is "Do it. Just do it!"

So it doesn't always matter how capable you *were;* making one-person decisions takes time, practice, an uncluttered head and a willingness to make mistakes regardless of who knows it. There are books galore, as I can testify, that give instruction and advice on how to list the pros and cons of any problem and judge the probability and possibility of a given solution. You can read them. Or you can make your list, close your eyes, and pick an answer. The important thing is, once you have taken into account the consequences of a decision, do not agonize—do it. Just do it!

Your common sense will return, and while you may continue to say "on the other hand," your self-confidence will grow with use. You have been making decisions all your life: You decided when to give your child an aspirin, the worth of a major appliance, and how to juggle job, family, assorted personalities, and household finances, as well as 101 other judgments. The arena seems frighteningly bigger now, but it's not that different really. You've already handled the role.

> *Making one-person decisions takes time, practice, an uncluttered head and a willingness to make mistakes.*

Emptying Closets, Emptying Drawers

"WHEN MY CHILDREN LEFT HOME I used to say that I hadn't lost a child, I had gained a closet. Now, it's all loss." This widow was speaking of the painfully sad task of parting with her husband's personal belongings.

Still, the great majority of widows would agree that going through their husband's clothes and possessions is a wrenching but therapeutic part of the grieving process. It's a small remaining vestige of the good-bye process people experienced when families prepared and buried their dead.

Avoiding that reality often boomerangs. "When I came home from the funeral, all his things had been taken out of the closet as though he had never lived there. My sisters thought they were doing me a favor, so I couldn't let them know how horrified I was. I felt so disloyal to Mike." The woman who said that, in describing the emptiness of her bedroom, wondered if she were peculiar. His clothes, she felt, were a part of him she wasn't ready to give up. Was that crazy? Morbid?

Absolutely not. Believing that out of sight is out of mind and that they are helping the widow accept reality, well-intentioned friends and family who try to erase the physical memory of a person all in one swoop actually deprive the widow of an important good-bye step. The time for saying good-bye to a worn tweed jacket, the shirt he always wore Sunday mornings, or a hardly worn pair of shoes may not be today; it may be many tomorrows away. It is not spooky to hold on to the presence of the man you lived with intimately for so many years. It *is* spooky, however, to come home to a sanitized bedroom. You will hear some women say they are grateful they were not subjected to the pain of emptying closets and packing up. "My children removed all his clothes. I couldn't face the thought," they say. But you will also hear resentment about not having been consulted about some item or other. And you will hear doubts whether "reality" and "acceptance" were improved by this bypass. Frankly, I believe the woman who waits for her own good-bye time before facing the reality of three drawers full of abandoned socks and underwear is better off in the long run. When she finally accomplishes that task she has made a statement: I will go on.

No Appropriate Interval

As for what is an appropriate interval for clearing the way, there is no set schedule. However, I do advise making some distinction between personal belongings and those artifacts of the joint household that will no longer be used or consumed and seem to be scattered all around. It is surely pointless to rub salt in the wound by surrounding yourself with the many reminders of a past lifestyle. These are best removed early and quickly.

Supposedly Queen Victoria continued to have Prince Albert's shaving accouterments brought in each morning long after his death. For several years, heartbroken and grief-stricken, the queen continued to act as though he were still present. And for those years afterward she could do little more than build monuments to Albert.

Among widows the subject of "my husband's clothes" ranks among the top ten.

Widows today also grieve and shed tears for their men, but his pipes, his ashtray, his after-shave lotion and other remainders need not become enshrined relics. No one is ever prepared for the sharp, sudden pain that the extra pair of eyeglasses posted near the telephone can evoke. Nor is anyone quite sure what to do with the paraphernalia that states, "Once my lover, my husband lived here." It is the little things the widow cries over: the half jar of his favorite bitter marmalade, his set of keys still in its key ring, the little white pad with the written reminder to call the accountant still on the desk.

Closets and drawers are more easily left closed for a better day. That task is usually approached within the first few months, but many people set the job aside for a long time. Among widows the subject of "my husband's clothes" ranks among the top ten. Both recent and longer-term widows say they still have things to give away. Most of us keep a shirt, a tie, a scarf or a sweater—something we can wrap around ourselves for occasional warmth and solace. I once admitted that I wore my husband's undershirts for nightshirts, and four out of 16 women in a widows-support group said they did, too. Four! But the point at which a widow literally moves her husband's material belongings from the space that is now hers alone is symbolically important. She is on her way to accepting the unacceptable although her way may not be always upward and onward in a straight line.

Quite typically, widows think they are behaving abnormally when they are either loath or unable to make a clean sweep of closets, chests and drawers within a month or so. One woman

Cleaning Out His Closets

The subject of "my husband's clothes" ranks high among topics of special concern to widows. Trust yourself to take this step when you feel the time is right—even if that is longer than other people expect. When you are having difficulty opening the door and looking inside, other widows variously advise:

- "Go ahead, break down."
- "Open the door and just look and touch."
- "Don't let it bother you; it took me seven months."
- "Every time I hear of a special cause or need, I bring a few things that I think can be used. Little by little I'm getting there. Do that."
- Ask another widow to help you box everything and then go out to dinner."

All good advice. The last suggestion points out that it often helps to have company for this particular job: family or someone understanding who will share the memories, stories and thoughts that come to mind and that you want to hear spoken. It makes it less lonely, too.

tearfully confessed, "My psychologist says I have to deal with my husband's clothes. It's been three months, but I still can't open the door to his closet." This woman was making herself crazy. In her head she had an exact picture of tasks and programs she expected of herself. She wasn't accomplishing enough. Her specific fear, it turned out, was that she would "break down" if she opened the closet door. The fear of losing control—not uncommon among new widows—had immobilized her.

It is comforting, and somehow important, to have even the most ordinary parts of the wardrobe put to good use. That may very well be why, lacking the right place and the right person, many women delay emptying closets and drawers. Once they settle that issue— giving items to friends, family, resale shops, the Salvation Army—the task becomes easier. However, the anonymity of the Salvation Army is less acceptable than directly passing on that nice turtleneck sweater and handsome leather jacket to a dear friend or relative. For different reasons, some children shy away from becoming heir to their deceased father's clothes. But the daughter who asks for a shirt to wear with jeans around the house and the son who keeps a tie for good luck on job interviews give as much as they receive.

Wheelchairs, eyeglasses, hearing aids, crutches, medical equipment, and, believe it or not, dentures are what many women have the most difficulty with. Loyalty? Guilt? They can't explain it, even though they know that their husbands held no fondness for those particular signs of their own failing. One woman waited a year before she could remove the crutches her husband had used for the last two years of his life to an outside storeroom, where they stood for another year before eventual disposal. Another woman held steadfast to the wheelchair her husband, a polio victim, had used all their married life: "That was his chair, part of the furniture."

These are just some of the dilemmas that are part of the process of letting go. They are not talked about in the average social gathering. Many subjects come up in a group of widows that would be beyond the tolerance of your nonwidowed friends. Not at all unusual is the widow who, after a year, is still debating what to do with cremation ashes—to have them buried, dispersed, or brought home—and who believes that she is the only person who has ever failed to act decisively in this matter.

Some women will try to maintain interests they never held or even disputed when they were a couple. Now they are listening to the country-western music they abhorred rather than the classical they enjoy, and watching TV sports programs they used to walk out on. Just another way of saying, "I wish you were here." They will hang on to a truck, a van or a wood lathe they will never operate, and that is not peculiar either. As any widow will tell you, "When the time is right. . . ." There is no time frame for the process of letting go.

Where you draw the line is hard to define, but clearly, if you are engaging in as-if behavior—as if he hadn't died—or in Queen Victoria-type behavior—building shrines—the sooner you drop the deception and get on with your own life, the better off you will be.

Start Small

There are no golden rules for how and when to let go, but there is a consensus among widows that advocates a sensible line between what to approach and what to avoid. Start with small, sensible steps, beginning with the more visible: the pills and toilet articles. Keep the after-shave lotion if you wish, but throw away the pills. (More than one widow has taken her husband's pills in that shadow stage of trying to hold on to an afterimage.)

Ask friends who offered unspecified help to help by canceling magazines, newspapers and memberships that are no longer relevant. When you are ready, tackle the clothes, books and all the physical leftovers of that other life. The valuable possessions, such as jewelry or other items that you wish to pass on or sell, may require more judicious handling. No widow need be swayed by demanding relatives, self-induced guilt or strictly sentimental considerations. The guideline to remember is: If the subject is difficult to speak about or the decision is hard to make, *wait!* The right time will come.

Dinner for One

"EAT," my aunt from New Jersey advised after my husband died. "Take care of yourself." And not only Aunt Sophie but your sister and your cousins and your children and the little voice in your head have also repeated that admonition. Good advice, but for the most part, dinner for one has little appeal.

For most people, breakfast and lunch are almost automatic functions. Our morning meal is usually ritualistic: coffee or tea preparation is like an extension of the arm—not much thinking is involved. The same for lunch. But dinner has to be planned. While there are cookbooks aplenty for that very contingency, and woks and slow-cookers in the back of the closet to facilitate the task, motivation must precede the recipe. Dinner has always been the meal for family, for two or more, and for conversation. It's no fun cooking for one; who's hungry?

There are, of course, the sensible people who watch their diet, prepare good meals, set the table and eat. From my observation point, though, that is not the norm. Here's what new widows do: They go a little berserk; they binge on snacks and get fat. Or they survive on TV dinners and get skinny. They fill the refrigerator with food that goes uneaten or they eat their way from peanut butter to pickles indiscriminately. They cook everything in one pot and eat out of the pot—in front of the TV. They don't plan meals; they eat what is on hand. Potato chips, canned tomato soup, chili, Oreo cookies and cottage cheese are the usual quick-fix numbers.

Dinner has to be planned.

So you know better. You know you should be eating a balanced diet and regular meals—sitting at the table and not standing over the sink. You know you should not be living off frozen meals, which are high in fat and salt, and snacks and drinks, with absolutely no nutritional value. Well, Aunt Sophie gave me some other advice that over the years has helped many widows overcome the dinner-hour blues.

"Don't think about it," she commanded. "Freeze individual portions of chicken, fish, hamburger. Slap one of them in a pan, bake a potato, fix a salad, and eat."

What Aunt Sophie so wisely concocted was a recipe that bypassed decision-making and self-pity, but went for the calories, vitamins and minerals. So let's back up a bit and fill in the spaces she left for you to fill in. To begin with, your good health is vital. One of the more frightening aspects of widowhood is who is going to look after me if I can't do for myself? Under stress we become careless about diet and indulge in some pretty crazy binges, sometimes out of ignorance, but often out of inertia.

Once I talked to a widower who ate a hamburger and French fries in the same little greasy-spoon restaurant every evening. He believed he balanced it off well because the meal included a so-called salad—iceberg lettuce topped with imitation dressing. That was ignorance; iceberg lettuce has about as much nutrition as three paper plates. And there was the widow who, nightly, surrounded two martinis with the contents of a doggie bag of leftover lunch. It wasn't too healthful to begin with—and she should have known better. It's bad enough to be a widow, but drunk and widowed? No one will love you, least of all yourself.

Even widows with children still at home are inclined to ease their standards; his presence is missed at the table. Often a takeout pizza or fried chicken becomes the standard meal more out of disinterest than any necessity. This may be a good time to involve the children in mealtime preparation and nutrition education.

Take Care of the Basics

A good basic diet should include plenty of whole grains, fruits and vegetables, and legumes. Add some fish, poultry and lean meats. But you do not require huge amounts as we used to think. Cut back on eggs, cheese, fats, sugar, caffeine and white flour. Pass on the fried foods and soda pop. Stay away from nitrates and chemicals. (I find it very easy to eliminate the latter just by reading labels.) For snacks, stay with nuts—not peanuts so much as almonds, low-cholesterol nuts and undressed popcorn, plus sensible amounts of fresh fruit. There is always a certain amount of controversy about vitamin and mineral supplements. Consult with a qualified nutritionist, either in person or through books. (In my experience, I've found that members of the medical profession have always underemphasized nutrition and that health-store operators . . . well, they have to pay the rent.) A good reference book is *The Jane Brody Good Food Gourmet,* which stresses good nutrition and fitness, along with both simple and gourmet cooking.

I suggest that, despite how passive about and uninterested in nutrition you may feel now, maintaining good health will ensure fewer problems in the long run. Don't buy junk foods. Fill your shopping basket with healthful essentials so when you're at the check-out counter you would not be embarrassed if my Aunt Sophie were standing behind you. In the beginning, many widows avoid cooking almost entirely and eat out more than at home.

Because they are uncomfortable about going to restaurants unaccompanied, they patronize fast-food places and cafeterias. Nothing wrong with that if the meals are balanced and healthful, but keep a suspicious watch for high-cholesterol cooking methods and preservatives that keep the vegetables brightly colored and vitamin-depleted. Later on, however, eating does become more of a social event as we make more friends and begin to fill our calendars with lunch with Annie and dinner with Barbara or Joe.

What most of us find out is that those who enjoy cooking do, after a while, fill their freezer and pots with creative cooking and overcome that initial impasse. And those who do not enjoy fussing about in the kitchen make greater use of modern shortcuts and judicious eating out. Until then, take care of yourself and eat right.

> *Fill your shopping basket with healthful essentials so when you're at the check-out counter you would not be embarrassed if my Aunt Sophie were standing behind you.*

It Seems so Real

"I'LL BE SITTING AT THE DESK, and suddenly I know he's in the room. I can *feel* his presence."

"I know I wasn't asleep, because I suddenly woke up and I could *feel* him sitting on the bed. I could *smell* his after-shave lotion. I touched his hand and said, 'Your hand isn't cold, but I know you're dead.' He just smiled and said good-bye. I didn't feel the least bit afraid."

"I know you'll think I'm crazy, but twice before I went to sleep I asked Barney to help me find some papers I had misplaced. In the morning I knew exactly where to look."

No, these women are not crazy or even unusual. When asked, a high percentage of widows—as high as 48 percent in one survey— say they have experienced the presence of their husband during the early months of bereavement. The presence may be just a feeling that he is there watching, encouraging and approving or may be clearly seen and heard. They don't bring up the subject in mixed company, of course, but when asked, and in the company of other widows, they report all kinds of paranatural and psychic episodes.

Many episodes they describe take place during the twilight period just before falling asleep or on awakening from a dream. The narrator may or may not be certain she was awake at the time but will describe the events in detail. These dreams are not easily forgotten. Most often the husband returns to give reassurance or counsel; occasionally to solve a problem. One woman, at an impasse about whether to sell her house or wait as everyone was advising, said her husband said to her in a dream, "Isabel, get the hell out of here," in such a loud, strong voice that she put the house on the market the next day.

Similarly, the woman who was debating about lending money to her son was set straight by her husband when he told her to refuse. "He's young, he'll manage. That's your security." Others would have given her the same tip, but coming from "the boss" himself it absolved her of any guilt.

However, sometimes nothing important transpires: "I heard him put the bowling ball away and say, 'Well, that was a waste of time.' And I said, 'What's new about that?' And then I turned over and slept the first good sleep I've had in two months."

Even those who entirely reject possibilities of the supernatural say they have heard words of advice and caution spoken so clearly that it was momentarily difficult to differentiate between reality and imagination. One woman said she was in the middle of asking the bank manager to explain why her check balance was incorrect when she heard her husband exclaim, "Just like my wife!" so loudly that she blushed. "I was sure everyone heard, but I realized it was just the echo of all those *my wifes* I had heard over the years. This time I wasn't annoyed with him, and I had to laugh."

Most of us can, and do, have an imaginary conversation with our husbands on any subject at the drop of a hat—his response to any given situation is known and predictable. My husband and I used to read the morning paper over breakfast in what I thought was silence. Yet for many months I could clearly hear his, "Oh God" as I made my way down the front page.

> *When asked, a high percentage of widows—as high as 48 percent in one survey—say they have experienced the presence of their husband during the early months of bereavement.*

For a time the widow will include her husband in actual conversations, but after a while becomes self-conscious about beginning a sentence with "As my husband would have said" and tries to delete those references. Nevertheless, she continues hearing those pronouncements, cautions and familiar phrases—often unbidden— forever. One woman called that *"the immortality of my opinionated spouse."*

One explanation given by disbelievers of voices attributed to the supernatural is that those outer-world visitations are only variations of sharp and painfully lingering memories in a troubled mind at a troubled time. This argument is countered with the claim that there are many ways of communicating that are unproved to us at present.

One theory offered, and which I totally reject, is that people born under certain zodiac signs are more prone to believe in such phenomena than others. That effectively takes care of people like me—Virgos—who are reputed to question not only visions from the other world but also astrology charts as well.

Dreams

Dreams, real dreams, are much the same at the beginning: very vivid, and again, with the good-bye theme running through. No matter how varied the script, most of the visions and dreams have one feature in common: They are comforting, surprisingly pleasant and oddly healing. "He came back for me the night after he died. We were laughing delightedly at our clever conspiracy, but all of a sudden I knew I couldn't do that to my children and I sent him away. We said farewell; I felt very peaceful. Honest to goodness, it was so real I was still smiling when I woke up."

> *Dreams have one feature in common: They are comforting, surprisingly pleasant, and oddly healing.*

Usually after a short time dreams such as these cease. For the most part, after some time has passed, most widows say that in their later dreams their spouse is usually alive and "just there." Widows say they are surprised how minor his role may be in the dream, as though nothing had changed. He never gets older, and is oftentimes younger. Sometimes, he even makes love. There is a mystical expectation for dreams, and some widows express distress when they haven't dreamed about their husband or are unable to conjure up a mental image of him at any time—day or night. Usually, that lasts only as long as the worry persists.

Dreams are funny. They sometimes give us more information than we want, and we subtly block them out. If you want to remember your dreams, you can. Keep a pad and pencil at your bed. With a little practice you can learn to wake yourself up and jot down the salient points of the dream before you go back to sleep. Come morning you'll be surprised how vividly the dream reassembles. Dreams have meaning for the dreamer; no one can interpret them better than you. Some counselors and therapists find them helpful in therapy and think dreams can be used productively to learn more about ourselves through the subconscious.

Dream books and Freudian symbols, on the other hand, don't have the answers, although a dream workshop that explores self-interpretations may prove quite interesting and informative. From all accounts, the most usual dream patterns in early widowhood have to do with letting go, anxiety about the times ahead, and, understandably enough, reliving happy periods associated with the past.

On occasion women have talked about escaping into dreams. One widow reported a recurring dream wherein she and her husband went out dining and dancing, and had wonderful conversations. Sleep was far better than being awake. At first she looked forward to the escape of nighttime, but after two months she grew frightened and spoke of her dreams to another widow. Whatever the reason, once she had talked about it, she never again had that dream.

Controversy about what is real, imagined, possible and impossible about the departed has not been resolved over the centuries. Most religions offer latitude for whatever you believe. Some hold out the hope for communicating and reunion after life. Most societies are tolerant and open to various theories and philosophies. You can probably find confirmation for whatever it is that you hold to be true—as I discovered at numerous widowed-persons' conferences.

Sessions on the subject of paranatural experiences and strange dreams are always well attended. Almost everyone in the audience has personal stories illustrating his or her belief and point of view. And many times when I moderated those discussions, I was surprised at how passionately some people believed in the dead returning. I must admit that I felt constrained to interject my own positive opinion. My tendency is to disbelieve those phenomena with the explanation that the parting of two people who have been as close as husband and wife goes on day and night in the conscious and subconscious. Then, from that basic state of mind, we do as we need to do. But that's just my opinion.

When to Be Careful

Just watch out for what others may be claiming. We have all seen the stereotypical widow exploited in staged seances where her husband returns with money messages, and we've heard of elaborate and expensive arrangements that were made for the return of a loved one. Houdini was supposed to have worked out a system whereby his wife would recognize him on returning. After many years she gave up; he never returned.

We hear and read many stories of widows who have spent good hard cash on phony promises. When a widow says, "I almost went out of my mind with grief," she may not be exaggerating. But don't confuse that with the common, everyday variety of contact that you will continue to feel when your spouse first dies, when you feel him still there, in the room, in the bed and hear his words in your ears and his love in your heart. You'll find that's a comfort—and right for the present.

Do I Answer the Mail?

WHEN SOMEONE WE LOVE DIES, we want that life acknowledged by others: Expressions of sympathy take on an importance that surprises most of us. The number of people who remembered, the quantity of cards and letters, as shallow as the messages may be, is more consoling than we ever imagined when we were the senders rather than the receivers. Don't laugh, but many widows can give you the exact count—knowing how foolish they are while they are counting. They can also give an accurate tally of those who neglected to write, knowing how futile that exercise is, too.

One woman, whose husband had been an executive of a large department store, was deeply hurt when the regional and the national heads of the corporation—men she knew only by name— failed to send personal notes. Paradoxically, as a former corporate wife, she could accept their impersonal code of ethics, but as a widow she felt their lack of sensitivity and caring. Illogically, this became the center of her grief for months.

Once received, however, cards and letters of sympathy can be, and are, an enormous emotional drain. The task of responding is not easily accomplished. Nevertheless, many widows feel it is their duty to answer each and every card—and do—while others see acknowledgments as an unnecessary formality, like writing a thank-you note in answer to a thank-you note.

Some people make a distinction between the printed, commercial cards they receive and personal notes, and answer selectively. Still others send out printed cards of thanks or place notices in newspapers, in the name of the family, to all who have in any manner paid their respects to the deceased. Then there are those who, a year later, are still facing a box of unanswered mail. Perhaps, as your mother used to say, "It's the way you were brought up."

Then there are the women who compulsively and immediately apply themselves to the task of writing individual answers to every message received. They reason that this is an absolute obligation of urgent priority. They see this task as part of the conventional funeral customs our society observes. It is their duty; to ignore that duty is unthinkable. Others disagree and feel no sense of urgency—or desire—to respond at a time when they have no heart for etiquette.

Often there is an overlooked friendship among the letters; reach for it.

If you want the advice of the majority in this, write notes to everyone who took time to write to you and don't feel obligated to answer the less personalized messages. If the correspondence is too heavy, write a personal letter that can be duplicated rather than the formal "The family of . . . wishes to thank you . . ." Although less personal, you can also buy printed cards with this message.

Respond to sympathy cards and letters within the first month. Your tears may dampen every note but those tears are cathartic. If you are overwhelmed, have friends and family help write some of the letters either in your name and signature, or theirs. Don't turn it all over to other people, though. You will find unexpected solace in connecting with the people who knew your husband and in some measure are sharing your grief.

Often there is an overlooked friendship among the letters; reach for it. An acquaintance, a widow I knew only casually through years of meetings and greetings at symphony concerts, wrote offering "to pick me up" for the next concert I felt like attending. We've been attending together ever since.

Involve Children, Close Friends

The children can answer those people known to them. As a joint family project, letter writing helps everyone. Good friends can lend a hand too. My close friend Helen appeared at my doorstep with a box of stationery under her arm one day after my husband died saying, "I came to help you with the correspondence and don't tell me never mind." My husband had been a well-known community leader, and the mail represented an imposing tribute with which I was gratefully burdened. Helen made notes about various people and wrote letters beginning: "Genevieve has told me about you, and I'm helping her thank some of her friends. . . ." Over the next few weeks we penned hundreds of letters together—often spotted with both our tears when someone recalled some special memory of my husband. It was good to have her company.

Rather than leaving that mail in the drawer and on the mind, answer the mail as best you can. It's part of mourning; it's part of accepting and consenting to reality.

> *Respond to sympathy cards and letters within the first month. Your tears may dampen every note but those tears are cathartic.*

Where Did I Put My Mind?

THERE MUST BE A HEAVEN FOR LOST PAPERS. Where else could they go? A well-shared symptom of "the crazies" experienced in early widowhood is the maddening amount of time spent looking for things you had in your hand only a moment ago, or had logically filed away for safe-keeping. You are sure you are going crazy: The check you were about to deposit is not on the hall table where you put it ten minutes ago, and the green form you were supposed to fill out and return a week ago turns up not green but pink, and not on the desk but in the linen closet with the towels.

Be assured you are not losing your mind; there are two other explanations. One is that papers and things have a life of their own, with heaven being a possible final resting place. The other is the theory of overload. You have much on your mind *Write down everything.* and several levels of conscious thinking going on at the same time. On the one level you are performing new and demanding tasks and making decisions, and on the other level you are trying to cope with your loss, your grief and the ever-growing realization of the full dimensions of that loss. No wonder the form turns out to be pink and not green. You are not going crazy—everyone seems to experience some memory loss and confusion during this period.

For such good reason the people who run funeral homes are organized and supply "guest books," those people-who-came lists (and what a burden those books are—impossible to throw away and not exactly what you want for your library). The funeral-home people really know about memory lapses and trust neither the weak nor the seemingly strong. They get everything in writing and give everything in writing. Take a cue from them.

Keep Records

Write down everything. Keep a log of messages, necessary tasks, phone calls with names of the people you talked to and all follow-up information. No matter how convinced you are that you will not forget, you probably will not remember that it was Darlene at the bank who was to call you back next Tuesday. You will come to believe that everyone is named either Darlene or Debby, only to find out there is no one with that name and no one has the vaguest notion of what you are talking about.

Without a file drawer or envelope for the estate records you will be a cooked goose at income-tax time. Meticulously file the vital records and expenses for that purpose. Not that you'll find things where you put them—or think you put them. Keeping track of important papers is difficult because you must not only recall where you filed them but also how you classified them.

Insurance receipts, for instance, might be under "I" for insurance one time and "T" for tax records another time. So make a cross reference when in doubt. Another thing: Use heavy, large letters on file labels. I've noticed myself that lost-paper heaven is a lot closer when I don't have my glasses on. A log similar to the phone log provides added insurance. Record the incoming mail and note its location, whether any follow-up action is necessary, and the date of completion.

You will improve your mental-confidence index if you maintain a ledger for expenses and income in addition to your checkbook. Sooner or later you will forget to enter a transaction in one or the other, and having a second record cuts memory lapses by half. Have a simple bookkeeping system. Besides being essential for the demands of our record-keeping bureaucracy, arithmetic—relearning the multiplication tables—will take your mind off other problems. A ledger will also help you establish a budget or at least

Having the actual numbers spread out in black and white on a page before you will free some memory cells for other anxieties.

provide an overview of how you are spending your money and of your fixed expenses. As a new widow, you will be worrying about money on consciously and unconsciously. You will find that having the actual numbers spread out in black and white on a page before you will free some memory cells for other anxieties.

Routinely write checks twice a month for your accumulated bills and advance payments. That's regular enough to keep you out of jail and to avoid late penalties.

Avoid piling paper upon paper. Make a decision and note with a Post-it® note what the final disposition is to be. Keep it simple and clipped together: TO BE DEPOSITED, TO BE ANSWERED, NEED TO CALL and so on. The successful executive never handles a piece of paper twice, they say. The distraught widow can't afford to because the chances for loss are increased each time.

Expect, at least once, that in paying bills you will send the electric company check to the phone company and vice versa. Compare notes with a 30-year-old who has just done the same thing and you will feel better. Don't fuss over bills on a daily basis. Routinely write checks twice a month for your accumulated bills and advance payments. That's regular enough to keep you out of jail and to avoid late penalties. Establishing a routine also means you will come across fewer odd envelopes in your purse that you forgot to mail.

A final word of advice: Check the wastebasket carefully before you dispose of your garbage. You may find a check or important document in the basket—but the envelope in which it came was left on the desk. New widows, of necessity, should have the most carefully scrutinized garbage on the block.

Oh, and did I mention the dirty cup in the refrigerator and the cottage cheese in the dishwasher? Don't worry, it happens to all of us.

Be sure to read the *Money, Money, Money* section in Part 2, page 123.

Hello, Who's Home?

IF YOU ARE THE AVERAGE WIDOW—middle 50s—no sooner have you adjusted to the empty nest than you suddenly have the whole tree to yourself. When the children left home the gap was filled, after a bit, with a comfortable change. There were fewer responsibilities, more time and freedom for the two of you to love, travel and focus on yourselves. But when the person who circumscribed your day is forever gone, who fills that gap?

Widows say the absolute bottom of desolation is coming home to the empty house. We all had our little rituals. "Hello, dear, I'm home," "Hi, it's me," and so on. My husband used to say, "Glad to see you," and the sound of those words continued to hang in the air long after I knew and accepted that I would never hear them again. It is little comfort—at the beginning—to hear that you will get used to coming home to your house and eventually will enjoy your privacy. But you do. I suppose it happens because we cannot go on forever minus a rudder and finally do evolve a plan for My Day rather than Our Day.

Creating a New Ritual

What survivors eventually work out is a new ritual, another kind of nonthinking routine. One widow said she would be eternally grateful to Peter Jennings. "Each evening Peter told me the news, and I told Peter what I thought of his news while I sipped a glass of wine. Anyone hearing me would have thought I was crazy, but when I said, 'Good night, Peter,' he answered me."

Others relate equally crazy routines to fill the void: singing to the plants, struggling through a 30-minute exercise tape, baking chocolate-chip cookies and giving them away, baking chocolate-chip cookies and eating them right away. And, of course, having intense conversations with the cat or dog.

Pets

While an animal, undoubtedly, is a great companion, some widows are resistant to taking on what they assume will be an additional responsibility or emotional risk. When a pet is already in place, that pet occupies a more important place than before, and losing Lady or Fluffy is doubly hard. When my Airedale, Tora, was killed by a car shortly after my husband died, and a few months later my tiger-striped cat met with disaster, I felt a close runner-up to Job. I carried a black cloud over my head for weeks. Tragedy would continue to rain on me; I knew it. Luckily, I had a friend who determinedly kept track of every new litter of kittens in the county and literally dragged me to choose between two tiger-striped kittens she had staked out for me. And, of course, being as indecisive as I was, I adopted both. The Katz brothers, as they came to be known, live and thrive, are big and fat, and we are cheered by each other's company. Not that one life replaces another; it simply adds on to another.

One woman I met told me she had a parakeet who greeted her enthusiastically with a five-minute conversation when she came home. Mostly the bird said, "My name is Charlie, what's yours?" And it always struck her funny that she answered, "Margery." I recommend pets, even goldfish. They're worth the trouble.

However, lacking something alive, many people leave a radio playing so they don't come home to silence. Silence is the villain. I once asked a roomful of widows how many kept the TV going, sometimes for as long as an hour at a time, without looking at it, and every hand shot up. Radio and music on CDs are what I prefer once I'm home. But, on coming

silence is the villain.

home, I never successfully managed to recognize the voice on the radio, which I'd left playing when I left the house. That ploy sounded like a good device against burglars, but it scared *me* every time.

Home Security

On the subject of burglars and home security, you can ease your mind considerably by having your house checked by a knowledgeable security person. In many communities the police department has such a service, free for the asking. A police officer will come to your house and advise you about locks (as will a good locksmith) and measures to be taken for better protection. The nice officer who came to my house had me trim a tall flowering quince tree close to the house because it offered such a good shield for an aspiring burglar or peeping Tom. He also helped organize a Neighborhood Watch program to cut down on the rash of burglaries in my section of town. I did feel reassured and less anxious after that. I also recall locking myself out a week after the locksmith had made every door and window "tight as a drum." I now have an extra key placed with a neighbor and another so well hidden even I can't find it.

Changing the Environment

Some widows find the ordeal of coming home can only be lessened with a complete physical change. They move to a smaller apartment, relocate, or in some tangible way make an effort to shed past associations. Visually that works, but most people are not that magically reconciled—or fooled. Some diversity in your environment will surely speed your taking full possession of your home: rearranging furniture or getting new slipcovers to better suit you, changing pictures, adding a dash of color with some fresh pillows, and especially decorating with live flowers and plants to catch your eye when you open the door.

In many communities a police officer will come to your house and advise you about locks and measures to be taken for better protection.

One of the simplest moves to be made is sleeping smack in the middle of the bed; no more his side and her side. I found nothing quite as depressing as the sight of my lonely imprint in the corner of my enormous king-size bed and few things more heartening than discovering that if it's good enough for a king it's good enough for a queen.

So begin with the less drastic and give it a fair try. You have to move in wherever you are. One day you'll make it, and one day you'll say:

"Hello, who's home?"

"Hello. *I* am home."

In Your Own Words

IN MY DAY, every adolescent girl kept a diary, and I was no exception. "Dear Diary, he looked at me today. He *really looked* at me! I nearly died." We wrote our secret thoughts and confidences. Most of us haven't turned to a diary since. We are more likely to seek out therapists and networks, or listen to ballads in times of emotional upheaval. In grief though, many widows return to their diary to give voice to pent-up, unspoken feelings at a time when their emotions and thoughts are unclear and acutely private. What is whirling around in one's head now is too new and immediate and too confusing for voicing. Keeping a diary—or *journal,* as they are now more often called—can be a lifesaver.

Start a Journal

Unless writing is an unbearable chore, every recent widow should try to start a journal of her thoughts and experiences. Frequency is unimportant, literary merit not necessary. Your early journal entries may be no more than the outpourings of your wandering subconscious and your tears on paper—even, perhaps, pages of aimless and pointless discourse. You'll feel better though, especially in the middle of the night, for having expressed yourself in quite a different way than with friends. "For the first few months," one woman recalled, "I couldn't sleep the night through. At two in the morning I'd be wandering around the house wide awake. Cookies and milk, hot baths, all-night talk shows. I even tried Spanish lessons on tape, which always made me sleepy during the day. Nothing worked until I started writing down what was on my mind, my worries, how I felt and what I had to do tomorrow. Then I'd go back to bed and immediately fall asleep."

Another woman said she wrote her thoughts in a notebook in the form of poetry and found that instead of unburdening herself when she was with other people, she saved her thoughts for a poem. That helped her as well as her fellow teachers, with whom she lunched everyday.

If you don't feel poetic, then swear, threaten and rant as necessary. One woman claimed her journal could have been X-rated. No one ever saw it, but then except for those few that are published, journals are rarely shared. A 78-year-old widow used loose-leaf pages and tore out her one-way debates with her son who she claimed was "dreadfully bossy" and would feel terrible if he ever knew how she felt.

> *"Nothing worked until I started writing down what was on my mind, my worries, how I felt and what I had to do tomorrow. Then I'd go back to bed and immediately fall asleep."*

No Instructions Necessary

No one needs instructions for journal-writing except that you will find it a help, and more purposeful, if you direct your writings to one person: yourself, Dear Diary, a real or fictional friend, or God, if you wish. Just so you have a sounding board and a way to speak openly in your own words. I wrote letters to my dead husband. My need to talk to him was overwhelming; there was no one else to whom I could expose that part of myself. At first I wrote to him every night when sleep was out of the question. The early entries were lamentations and entreaties. "Dear Martin," I wrote, "Everywhere your clothes are still mingled with mine—in the hamper, in the hall closet; your sunglasses still fall from the sun visor when I make a left turn. Everything is still ours. There is too much for me. I took a walk this morning in your jacket. The early air was clear and moist, green from all of the world. You must be part of the morning; I feel you there."

A week later: "The leaves are falling from your fig tree—big and yellow—dry before they reach the ground. In less than a day the tree is almost bare. Clinging hard are some green figs. They will never ripen, not even the birds will eat them. Will I ever blossom and bear fruit again? I feel dead."

And months later: "See what I've learned: how to open a sticky dresser drawer, to take a mechanical puzzle into the light of my limited reason, to fix a leaky toilet, to understand that I lost my way on a road because I never thought to observe the north and south of the road. Why did you indulge my ignorance?" And, "Today, for the first time, the desert felt friendly under my feet—no longer hostile—when I walked alone."

Then, later, "Why did you keep all your records in that wonderful head? Who is Jacob C. Lake; what does this paper mean? The phone didn't ring once tonight, I've been deserted. No, *you* deserted me, *your* friends have forsaken me. . . ."

Still later, "I and the car got stuck in three feet of water going over the Dodge Road bridge tonight. It was raining floods—I was meeting Rachel and Jean for dinner—and I went through the water just as you always did, thinking that the old Mercedes could clear the Red Sea, just as you always said. Well, it didn't. Before I could even panic, a voice came out of the wet, dark night from a car behind me, 'Steer ahead, Mrs. Ginsburg, I'll push you across.' It was Joe, who used to have the vegetable market where we always bought our grapefruit years ago. He had recognized the car, and it seems, also knew about you. We left the car in the parking lot right off the bridge, Joe drove me to the restaurant, and later, after dinner, Rachel and I returned. The rain had stopped, the car was dry and started right up, and I was so pleased with myself that I returned via the Dodge Road bridge without a second thought. (The water was down, of course.) Now I'm asking myself, Did you send an angel (in the form of Joe) to rescue me, or was it your fault that I went over the bridge in the first place? And you know what I think? It's my life, not yours—for credit or blame. But you know that, don't you?"

> *"See what I've learned: how to open a sticky dresser drawer . . . to fix a leaky toilet, to understand that I lost my way on a road because I never thought to observe the north and south of the road. Why did you indulge my ignorance?"*

A Progress Chart on Coping

One day I reread my letters. Before me was a clinical progress chart on coping: at first, anguish and confusion; next, anger and resolution. And now, unbelievably, I read more comedy than tragedy, more hope than despair. Look, I was boasting unabashedly about accomplishments so minor that a 10-year-old would have pooh-poohed them. Not that my emotional progression was that steady or constant. It was my returning objectivity that surprised me; my focus was no longer centered solely on my loss. I was overcoming. Nothing that I had done, or was to do, pumped me with more reassurance than this visible evidence of my survival. I was making it, I read it right here. You'll find some of those letters at the end of each section, beginning with the journal entry following this chapter.

Eventually my letters ended and evolved into companionable travel journals and little commentaries in my weekly appointment book—but addressed to me. Sometimes I keep them, sometimes I don't. Writing down my impressions and personal thoughts is an affirmation of my life, it seems to me. It's an acknowledgment of a fact of life: I alone am my best friend now. I still sometimes "think" a Dear Martin letter—and I guess I always will. But that's normal, isn't it?

It was my returning objectivity that surprised me; my focus was no longer centered solely on my loss. I was overcoming.

A Journal Entry

Firsts

Dear Martin,

This has been a time of "firsts." So many, and each one stands out like a milepost for me; to anyone else it's hardly a pip. Perhaps even you wouldn't have noticed anything remarkable about my picking up a mouse by its tail from the pool, putting air in a tire (Why does it always hiss?), or climbing to the roof to unplug a drainpipe. But you would have noticed that I didn't call you.

Tell me, how did I get to be this old without ever buying stock— we always discussed it, but you dealt with it—recording a deed at city hall, firing an insurance agent or appealing our house assessment? All of these firsts I take some pride in, as you can tell. But not so with the first lobster dinner I ate without you, the first perfect, triple rainbow across the eastern sky we didn't share, and several delightful movies you would have cheered. I keep thinking the second time won't be so hard—but I've lost my taste for lobster, I notice.

What I'm really writing you about is coming home last night. I had been at a two-day biofeedback conference in Phoenix and then flew up to Crested Butte to meet Ann and two new women friends you don't know for a weekend of cross-country skiing. Two firsts in that: a vacation without you and the cross-country skiing. I did fine. I can see your grin at the sight of me both upright and downhill after everyone had written me off as permanently upside down.

No, it was coming home I was unprepared for. The first time in 30 years that either we were not together or you were not there at the airport to meet me. Now that's crazy, why were you always there waiting; how is it that I never before went unmet? But I didn't—this was a first. People waving, jumping up and down, talking excitedly, kissing, hugging. And for me—nobody. What a cold plunge into reality. "Don't think, just walk ahead, pick up your luggage, go home. That's the way it is. See, look over there, there's another woman all alone. Nothing wrong with her."

Today I have the feeling that I've done it all now; that I'm ready for "seconds." Coming home to not find you waiting for me at the airport was my first rite of passage. I can't depend on you to be there anymore.

Love,

Me

Part 2

Rebuilding Your Life

IS THERE AN EXACT MOMENT when you chose to live, or accepted that, willing or not, you would go on with your life? Some widows say yes, they can remember a turning point, a conscious awareness of stepping forward over the line. It might have been symbolically, in a dream, or when the first sliver of humor invaded their anguish. However you came to decide to go on with living, that is what you are doing now. Some social scientists cavalierly call this period the *transition from grief to acceptance*. Sounds easy, but as you know, you don't get there on greased wheels. If we need to have a label, the *period of reconstruction* is more apt: Build, fall down, rebuild.

Now that your despair is not as constant, every now and then a glimmer of promise comes, from within yourself, unexpectedly. Friends and family are back in place, you are more alone than ever in your life, but there is a growing realization that is beginning to separate you from the past. Your sense of yourself is changing. You don't know who you are and what you want, but you no longer feel so helpless. Going ahead is like that: full of unknowns, conflicting emotions and piercing discouragements. All are mixed with the triumph of accomplishments that make you feel so proud of yourself you could fly.

That's why this section begins with the many configurations of depression and sadness. You may wonder why this topic has been so long in coming because your every day has been marked with sorrow. The reason is, you expected to grieve and so did all your friends and family. You needed no rationale. But now, allowing yourself to be sad and allowing yourself to be happy may be less acceptable to you and to them. I hope not. So we begin with a reminder that depression is always normal and so is happiness.

And now that you are beginning to captain your moods, you are also confronting many other issues and tough facts of life on your own. The remainder of this section explores your changing relationships with people, things and yourself.

In the desert canyons and mountains where I live, I often see a flower miraculously growing from a rock—with no crack to anchor it, no soil to nourish it—because it is a survivor. You may not see yourself quite so metaphorically. But, take it from me, flowers do grow from rocks.

The Blues

LOOK UP *depression* in the dictionary and you'll find synonyms like *melancholy* and *dejection*. Look up *sadness* and you'll find *grieving* and *mournful*. Most widows would never notice a difference between these definitions. If there is a normal response to the death of a spouse, most would report feeling at least five degrees below average on any measure used.

The word *depression* has a psychiatric sound. After all, depression is an extension of the normal processes. And unless it reaches clinical proportions we all know it well. There are times when we feel that getting out of bed is not worth the effort. That's not new, because life is full of those days. Depression, according to my simplistic theory, follows when you hear, "No! You can't have it. No, you can't do it. No!"

With the death of your spouse you have just heard the definitive "no." What is new is the feeling of unending desolation at the very time when you no longer have the sharer of black moods and uplifter of low spirits at your side. The dialogue of "What's the matter?" "Nothing," thrice repeated until at last you tell what is on your mind, is now an irredeemable, solitary monologue. Hard as it is to believe, that desolation does end. Depression and sadness, to some degree, go on forever, much as they did before. Unlike in the past, however, these low moods and tears may last and reappear for much longer than either we or those around us expect. That's because this loss is not transient, not reversible. It is during these periods that we and also our friends and family wonder if our depression is normal.

Usually it is. Clinical depression—to get that out of the way—most often occurs in those who have had a predisposition for that problem in the past. Typically, that person will not interact with others and will have ongoing sleep and appetite disturbances, sometimes with suicidal thoughts. When the intensity and duration, and impact on daily functioning are severe, professional intervention is indicated. Psychiatrists agree that medication is overwhelmingly effective in severe clinical depression.

However, some of those same symptoms may appear in the so-called *normal* person when a loss as significant as the death of a spouse occurs. But the depression is to a far lesser degree and for a briefer period of time. Then it is not a medical problem—and that is what confuses people. You are likely the best judge of your own emotional stability during this period.

Some widows, do believe medication helped them endure their grief. "I don't think I would have lived without those pills at the beginning. They helped me sleep at night and get through the days during the first six months." But others, and easily a majority, feel just the opposite. As painful as it was, living the sadness, knowing the depression, kept their senses alive for also experiencing peace and joy later on. "I gained strength from hanging in there. I alone had to do it." No one has ever suggested, however, that the sadness lifts quickly and permanently all by itself—with or without pills.

Ups and Downs

People are often fooled into thinking that grief moves out steadily; every day a little better. When it doesn't, they immediately assume something is wrong. All widows do not cope with loss in the same manner. Someone who never developed a mature response to loss may never have learned how. The deposed queen—the woman whose husband elevated her to a special niche and waited on her hand and foot—has a tough time now that she no longer is in control of her kingdom. And the very-dependent woman faces a trying readjustment because she has little practical experience in surviving life's little problems, let alone this major one. In general, those who have weathered other crises cope better, although there are no limits to the surprises one sees among widows. Nevertheless, the best of women who cope is likely to be more depressed than she ever has been before. She may find that grief is only relieved by grieving.

That may sound like a glib recipe. More than one widow has complained, "They tell me I must go through my grieving, but I don't know what they mean."

Grieving Out Loud

In answer to that, an experienced widow once advised, "Don't do what I did—be cheerful no matter how I really felt and never speak of my husband. I thought speaking of him made my friends uncomfortable. I think grieving means that you allow yourself to feel absolutely lousy without being too concerned about how it looks to others."

Other widows, also from hindsight, interpret grieving in terms of caveats: what *not* to do. One widow, whose husband had regularly traveled on his job, went on as though he were away as usual; she played daily at her tennis club and attended club parties. According to her account, she was not available for sympathy or a change in roles. "I didn't want to be a typical widow, I wouldn't allow myself to act like one or feel like one," she said. "That was the most depressing thing I ever did in my life." Other widows counsel to allow one's sadness to prevail rather than masquerade as a cheerful faker. No one is urging that you parade your sorrow and make your grief the centerpiece at every table, but constant pretending is wearisome for you—and your audience.

> *Other widows counsel to allow one's sadness to prevail rather than masquerade as a cheerful faker.*

The wisest prescription lies somewhere in the middle: composed of one part self-pity, one part acceptance and one part sheer grit. The world is filled with widows who, in spite of being ill-prepared for the management of their own lives and affairs, make an unexpected adjustment. That's where the grit comes in. However, the woman who masks her feelings and denies herself the reality of sadness will blossom only when all that grit is watered down with tears. Acceptance is the real joker, though. Too much acceptance implies denial and too little of it results in inappropriate anger.

The trick of balancing anger takes a lot of trial and effort. Hardly anyone does it perfectly. Result? One more good reason for depression, sadness and feeling low. Psychologists say that internalized anger is the reverse side of the depression coin. Historically, women have been the peacemakers; their relationships with males so frequently have depended on their being second in line. As widows they are often more comfortable feeling sad and helpless rather than angry and assertive. It's a habit.

The Rubber-band Test

Check it out with the rubber-band test. Wear a good, stout rubber band around your wrist for one week. Snap it hard every time you blame yourself or pick on yourself. "I did it badly." *Snap!* "I'm so stupid, I'll never learn." *Snap!* "I'd better keep my mouth shut, I'm probably wrong." *Snap!* "No one cares about me. Why should they?" *Snap!* "I shoulda, I coulda, I woulda." *Snap, snap, snap!* If you find your wrist red and tender, you have a clue to the cure: Stop mistreating yourself. Keep your rubber band in place until you break the habit. Stop turning your anger inward with self-blame, self-deprecation and all the other little nay-saying devices that you've used forever. You will feel more in control of your life, less helpless and consequently less depressed.

Alternately, the woman who expects a great deal of herself, to be in control of situations and, in general, to be able to cope better than your average widow will also lapse into a kind of depression denial. She can't lower her expectations or yell "Help!" And after months or years of model coping, anger gets caught in the cracks and emerges as the blahs. This is like our tennis widow and those who think it is a sin to feel sorry for themselves. We all go through phases when we are just plain tired of coping. Regardless of how competent and independent we have become, we long for a little dependency. It's when the crystal ball foretells nothing and comes up all no's. So we have a temper tantrum.

Nonproductive Expressions of Grief

Too big to lie on the floor and scream and kick, we engage in equally nonproductive and self-hurtful antics: boredom and disinterest in usual activities. "No thanks, I don't feel like doing anything" is a tantrum. Rampant apathy is a tantrum. Eating until you feel fat and sloppy is also symptomatic. Some take a stab at martyrdom by denying themselves anything that might be entertaining, interesting or involve the expenditure of money; they are suddenly poor. Worst of all is alcohol and drugs. Remember the six-month syndrome? Although by no means limited to that time frame, many widows experience this kind of letdown after six months. Having survived the terrible tasks and initial grief of widowhood there is a lessening of structure. There are fewer required projects, fewer people who rally 'round, and fewer pats on the back from others and from yourself. Is this the way it will be forever?

> *Widows say, exercise aside, keeping busy is the best way to dispel depression.*

Exercise, Keeping Busy Helps

After a time you will come to recognize temper-tantrum depression. Physical activity will break the mood. You can check that out by literally forcing yourself into action. I've found it's impossible to jog, hike, swim, do aerobics or even do deep breathing and be depressed at the same time. Most of the hiking and hard walking I do now is recently learned, so age is no barrier. You can hit golf balls from a wheelchair.

Widows say, exercise aside, keeping busy is the best way to dispel depression. They also add that aimless activities—no goals, no plans, no commitment and no inner satisfaction—serve no purpose and even increase despondency. You may be surprised by the outcome of a project you undertake. One woman engaged in collecting family history and memorabilia for her son's fortieth birthday and was delighted when she was able to use this experience to teach a related course at the local junior college. The point is that there are many aspects to "keeping busy." Busyness doesn't find you, however; you have to find *it*.

Still, the "busy" formula does not work for everyone. "When I'm feeling bad I don't want to talk to anyone or see anyone. I just want to be miserable, and I've learned that it will pass if I don't fight it. It's okay to be miserable." Those words express a sentiment shared by many seasoned widows. To carry it further, they add that, as with insomnia, if you don't worry unduly about feeling blue it's not so disturbing. If you let it be, and don't wallow in it, the blues will become just plain boring.

Finally you say, "The heck with this," pull up your socks, go forth and *just do it*. It can't be repeated too often: depression, sadness and feeling hopelessly miserable is a normal reaction to the death of a loved one. It's also a normal reaction to living.

Now you may expect to feel worse than ever anticipated, and over a longer period of time may encounter that feeling with periodic, unreasonable valleys and hills. Don't hesitate to see someone if you want counseling or medication, but know what you're feeling is normal and par for the course.

And remember: Be kind to yourself.

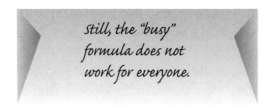

Still, the "busy" formula does not work for everyone.

To Wear or Not To Wear Your Wedding Ring

TO WEAR OR NOT TO WEAR a wedding ring is not just a question with widows; it is a raging debate among married couples. Nothing so represents marriage as the wedding ring—for better or for worse.

Most psychotherapists and counselors advise widows that in removing their wedding bands they are accepting the reality of death and the beginning of a new phase of their lives. The ring, the symbol of marriage, is better put aside after the death of one of the partners, they say. Intellectually, most widows agree. Emotionally, they chicken out.

"I thought I would never part with my ring, no matter what I heard," commented one widow, "I was forever married, but one day about six months after Tommy died, I looked at my finger and realized that it was no longer true; I had no husband. The ring had to come off so I could say good-bye not only to him but to that which was."

From another, "I had to get angry before I could pull that wretched ring off. It took soap and Vaseline®. For months and months I didn't believe I had the right to be angry but, boy, did I make up for lost time. Our affairs were in such a mess. I almost threw the ring away, but of course I didn't—it's a diamond band."

Many a widow has removed her ring not once but several times. "It didn't seem right. I thought people would think me callous, so I wore it again for a long time," one woman explained. Or what is just as common: "My finger felt so bare, I couldn't get used to it at first."

There are just as many good reasons for keeping the ring in place. Loyalty to one's marriage and spouse is, of course, the dominant one. "I will be wearing my ring when we are reunited" is often heard. The less adamant see the whole issue as unimportant: "Why bother? I don't intend to get married again," and, "After 46 years, the ring is part of my hand."

Protection from unwanted male attention is sometimes given as the reason for wearing the ring. In truth, underlying a good part of the reluctance of widows to desymbolize their left hand has to do with status. The older woman still retains the belief that the term *widow* is better than *spinster*. In the words of one woman, "I put a lot of hard work into getting this ring, and I'll be damned if I'm going to give it up so quickly." That side of the case is irrefutable.

Widows, like everyone else, worry about the good opinion of those around them: whether they will be considered disloyal or to be signaling their readiness for fun and frolicking before an appropriate lapse of time. Not too long ago, those who could afford the more elaborate black trappings of widowhood wore a black-banded ring for a year as part of their widow's weeds, thus providing clear direction. I would not be surprised if one day some enterprising jeweler revived the custom.

The total lack of ritual and custom connected with death in our day leaves us awash in decisions and dilemmas. In the case of the wedding ring, widows have to deal with their own sentimentality, and let's face it, also the groaning absence of ritual to mark the passage. Taking the ring from the left-hand ring finger is unsettling.

A time comes when we want to step into a new experience without the burden of ghosts.

Widows who remove their wedding bands don't forget that occasion any more than they forget when it was originally slipped onto that same finger.

Most will tell you—and this holds true for widowers as well as widows, although men come to this point sooner and with less struggle—that the day comes when we no longer feel married. A time comes when we want to step into a new experience without the burden of ghosts. At first the thought of casting off something as integral a part of our union as our wedding ring is inadmissible, not even an issue. Gradually, in the process of parting, the thought becomes not only acceptable, but logical—for some, at least. For others, never. If you are of two minds, move your ring from your left hand to your right, or wear it on a chain around your neck—as some do. Perhaps you are not ready. Wait.

Your wedding ring, in the final analysis, is a link to your own memories—to be worn or remembered as you please.

The Ring: Other Tried-and-Tested Options

There are all shades of gray; you might consider some other uses for your wedding band. A few alternatives are mentioned below.

- You can refashion your engagement and wedding rings into a new ring.

- You can have your band and your husband's melted together into a new piece of jewelry. Many have done this. This idea preserves the sentimentality you associate with this jewelry and your continuity with the past.

- Not to be passed over is the alternative of saving your ring for the next child or grandchild planning to marry. A lovely sentiment, but be aware it is one not always shared by other generations. You do have to brace yourself for a possible difference of tastes.

Yesterday a Wife,
Today a Mechanic

THE LAW OF THE WIDOW states that during the first year of widowhood three major appliances shall break down—successively. You may substitute *roof, automobile, plumbing*—yours or that of your house— for the word *appliance*. Whether you're a homeowner or apartment dweller, the law will get you in the end, somehow. (I'm sure you don't want to hear about the widow who lost the cap on her front tooth on the day of the funeral, let the water run over in her bathtub onto the ceiling below two days later, and shortly thereafter, was burglarized. Just imagine if she'd had major appliances!)

Refuting the validity of the widow's law are those who claim that widows are not necessarily being persecuted; they simply are at the low ebb of tolerance and response. In the past, three breakdowns in a row, the sages insist, were treated as single nuisances. "We've had that dishwasher for quite some time," your husband would remind you, and you would call the repairman without any trace of paranoia.

While it's a good idea to be prepared for disaster, at the same time don't court it unnecessarily. That is just as bad. Recent widows often have a way of waving their magic wands in reverse: they look for trouble. They begin to worry about "what-ifs" and somehow succeed in gaining the complete cooperation of both equipment and mender.

To illustrate: There are refrigerator watchers who hold their breath waiting for the motor to go back on every time the cycle goes off. Just checking—until finally, the darn thing obliges. There are the flat-tire anticipators who are reluctant to drive outside the rear-mirror view of a garage. In the end, they replace all four tires for peace of mind. And in the hot, dry climate where I live, there are the roof worriers; among those widows the subject of roofs always comes up. The names of reliable roofers are passed around like gumdrops. One thing about roofers is that they'll always find something that needs to be fixed.

It is not difficult to discriminate the real from the imagined, though. When something doesn't work you know it. Nevertheless, even then, it pays to take another look just to certify that you're not gazing at your latest self-fulfilling prophecy. Keep your appliance manuals handy and read the troubleshooting instructions. Usually you'll find a checklist, and sometimes it is a simple thing like a disconnected plug complicated by your own panic. Maybe there's a reset button. Air-conditioners, garbage disposals and other motorized paraphernalia have circuit breakers that turn off the power when the motor overheats. The reset switch is usually red. Push it in, it's in the directions somewhere. If it's still not working, try a little kick and jiggle the switch. No?

Then call a serviceman. Describe the problem, ask for a cost estimate, travel-time charges, guarantees and availability. Call two others and compare. You will feel like the person in charge and not the victim of the machine. Never indicate to unfamiliar workmen that you are living alone; create a full-house impression. I usually make some gratuitous comment like, "Oh, we are going to be so glad to have the furnace working." You may even go as far as one of our ladies, who calls progress reports to her nonexistent husband who is supposedly working in the nonexistent study. Use the same precaution away from home when you are arranging for delivery or repairs. Don't mention that you live alone, that your husband recently died, and that you need something reliable, as one woman did when shopping for a used car. Don't begin a sentence with "I'll be away on vacation. . . ." Should you hear yourself slip, follow with a fast cover-up such as "but my son is next door."

> *Never indicate to unfamiliar workmen that you are living alone; create a full-house impression.*

Get a Second Opinion

Whenever possible, get a second opinion—for cars, sometimes three. I once had all the 220-volt electrical equipment in my house go out. The electrician I called (from the Yellow Pages) diagnosed the problem to be a faulty underground wire under the foundation. "We're gonna have to get a jack hammer in and dig her up," he told me. I saw my life's savings pass before my eyes as digging it up also included my beautiful brick floors. Fortunately, the words, *second opinion* also flashed before me. The next electrician found the trouble to be in the electric company's connection—overhead— which was the company's repair, not mine. That experience taught me two things: to regard all so-called *experts* with more suspicion than veneration, and that there are no electrical wires under my house.

Another time, when the driveway needed repaving, I learned a fortune of facts from the estimators; they love to talk. By the time the five bids (I was perhaps a bit excessive) came in, I knew all about single-coat, double-penetration, pea gravel, chip-and-seal, cold asphalt; I knew exactly what to specify in the contract because one estimator would always warn me about how the other guy might cheat me. A whole new area of expertise; I wrote in my journal, "Today I paved the driveway."

You'll Become the Expert

As you go along you will also learn a good deal more than you ever wanted to know. Pick up one of those basic household-repair books that cover everything from changing light bulbs to how to rebuild a toilet's flushing system.

What you can't learn from the books you can sometimes learn by watching the repair person. Some women become so proficient at repairs and maintenance they're able to climb a ladder to repair the roof as easily as they used to flip a pancake. One widow got so good she gave her bridge club a lesson on rewiring table lamps, followed by

Pick up one of those basic household-repair books that cover everything from changing light bulbs to how to rebuild a toilet's flushing system.

instructions for changing the oil in a car. With a few good tools you can easily replace a washer to fix a dripping faucet, replace a faulty electrical plug on any appliance cord and connect a VCR.

Have These Tools On Hand

There are a few vital items that every woman who lives alone should have:

- ✆ hammer
- ✆ two screwdrivers (flat and Phillips)
- ✆ adjustable wrench and knife
- ✆ flashlight
- ✆ candles
- ✆ baking soda near stove for grease fires
- ✆ spare fuses if you have a fuse box
- ✆ a small fire extinguisher
- ✆ a connected garden hose outside if you are a home dweller
- ✆ a well-stocked first-aid kit with aspirin
- ✆ a can of WD-40® oil, which eases, loosens, prevents and makes things work
- ✆ If you find yourself especially handy, you might want to add an electric drill and who knows what else?

Electricity and Plumbing

For electrical repairs: Don't touch any wires and never do what I once did—stand ankle-deep in water and disconnect the swimming-pool-filter motor. You never know which of your nine lives you're working on. The novice should stick to learning where the fuse boxes are, what fuse goes to what, and how to reset them. Of course, if you live in an apartment house you need only learn how to press the proper buzzer. Eventually, although getting it to happen takes skill too, a superintendent comes running. For smaller electrical repairs, anyone with a desire to learn can connect a new appliance plug and rewire a lamp. But until you get the knack, have someone check it. Periodically check for frayed wires. Never use a light-weight extension cord for heavy equipment or high-watt bulbs in fixtures that specify low wattage.

As for plumbing: The greatest contribution you can make in any plumbing emergency is to know how to shut off the water. In your house there is a main water shutoff valve. Locate it and practice turning it off and on. You may need a special tool to turn it. If it sticks, here's where the WD-40 comes in. The shutoff is what you turn when water gushes out of a broken pipe and you can't find a closer individual shutoff. It is what you turn off when checking the water meter and what you casually point to when the plumber asks, "Where's the shutoff, lady?" Get to know it—this valve is your friend.

Become familiar with the individual shutoff valves leading to sinks and toilets.

Also, become familiar with the individual shutoff valves leading to sinks and toilets. Again, prepare them for easy turning; if your husband had a very firm grip you could become very perturbed with him if you should ever have the unhappy experience of having the toilet *not* stop running when flushed. For such emergencies, immediately reach for the shutoff valve and turn clockwise. Continuous running water in the tank, but not flooding, can often be corrected with minor adjustments (adjusting the float, replacing the flapper) that are explained—with diagrams—in your handy repair book. Easy!

You can get great satisfaction from acquiring these mechanical skills. Of course there are plenty of women who have been handy all along, but for most of us that was our husband's domain: "Dear, while you're taking out the garbage, notice how that door is squeaking." Part of our early panic results from wondering how we will be able to manage without that neat division of responsibility. Too bad it took us this long to find out that the garbage wasn't that heavy and a little WD-40 unsqueaks anything. Well, after all, he didn't know how simple it was to fix a meat loaf.

Or Find a Good Handyman

For the faint of heart, it is perfectly all right to put your whole effort into locating a good handyman. As one widow said, when she was teased for bringing her car in for repairs because transmission fluid was leaking from the rear—only to find out it was coming from an uncapped can she had left in her trunk—"After all, I'm not a mechanic. If God had wanted me to be one I would have been born with a screwdriver in my hand."

For her and other women—with and without screwdrivers in hand—if you learn nothing else, memorize the words of the wise man who wrote, in soap, across the bathroom mirror for his wife to see:

LEFT IS LOOSE, RIGHT IS TIGHT!

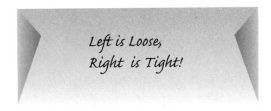

Family Relationships

I USED TO HAVE A PSYCHOLOGY PROFESSOR who periodically punctuated his explanations of the human condition with "Nothing is forever." No one knows that better than the widow, because suddenly nothing is the same. Change comes with a jolt and a crash, and like an earthquake, never quite settles back into its original place.

Among the more noticeable changes are those involving family connections. Most widows say that their family circle, while it has grown smaller, has grown closer, more caring of each other. But few would deny that even at best, subtle changes do take place and that relationships are never as they were. One falling leaf forever alters the tree. With families, each relationship has individually changed and has had a rippling effect, with no beginning and no set ending.

What happens? Why do children act like parents, parents act like children, sisters act like brothers, and brothers act like chairmen of the board? What has happened, first of all, is that you have changed. You are more vulnerable, more sensitive, more confused, more angry and more afraid, to name a few of your new, unwanted acquisitions.

You are more vulnerable, more sensitive, more confused, more angry and more afraid.

Very likely, you are also trying to be brave and independent. You feel out of balance with the world and, in fact, you are. And, if you are not the same, consider that others are responding out of their own new feelings and thoughts as well. So, indeed, the family circle is closer but at times more of a squeeze than we'd like. Let's take a look at some of the problem areas. If you have none, read on anyway, and feel lucky! But if you belong among the majority of widows, you will find something familiar in these selected scenarios, or as one woman labeled our soap-opera lookalikes, "As the Stomach Turns."

Children May Be Protective

At first everyone rallies around Mom. Because the widow is the center of sympathy and concern, her children act out society's expectations. We can't do anything that might upset mother, they think, and mother from her corner doesn't wish to impose her inner turmoil on her children. It's after the funeral, and everyone is still speaking in formula.

"Sell the house, what do you need such a big house for?"

"Don't do anything for a year."

"Take a trip."

"You'll always be welcome in our house, Mom."

"Don't worry about Dad's clothes, we've moved
 everything out."

"Please be sure to eat, Mom. I've put six pizzas and ten
 frozen dinners in the freezer."

No one dares speak her or his thoughts lest they seem too terrible and too self-interested—which they often are. Consequently, the true words and real feelings may never be sorted out, or worse, they will be left unspoken when silence is not the better part of wisdom. The most frequently expressed sentiment among widows is: "My children are wonderful, but they have their own lives to live."

Does that mean you visit by invitation only? Does that mean you don't call your son to look at the washing machine when it quits? That you wait for the children to phone *you?* (This is a big issue for some.) That you don't know whether they really want you to spend a week at the Cape with them or they're just doing their duty? That you should always answer "Fine"

> Because the widow is the center of sympathy and concern, her children act out society's expectations.

when they ask how you're doing? Head thoughts! You think that's what they think, they think that's what you think, and what we call *communication* never takes place. In a typical true example, the daughter-in-law of a widow of three weeks invites her for dinner. "And we'd like you to have dinner with us every Friday night," she adds.

The widow, while mumbling a polite, grateful acceptance, is already thinking, "Does she mean it, is that *her* idea, is it my *son's* idea, should I wait for her to call me next Friday, do I want to do that, do they?" Here is a relationship on the threshold of change.

Right from the time of their father's death the children are going through private grief and their separation from a parent. The daughter, once the little princess to her daddy, has lost her royal place, and possibly her financial security if she is still in school or not yet on her own.

Daughters, often more tuned in to their mother's emotions than sons, hardly feel free to share their own self-interests with their mothers, yet at the same time are themselves frustrated givers. "I don't know what to do for my mother. I call her from New York every week, and she says she's all right, but I know she isn't." It's a silent conversation.

Sons, willingly or unwillingly, are expected to take care of mother. They are not expected to add their tears to hers or be resentful of what is certain to become an additional responsibility. The old "Be a man" refrain, in one form or another, is always being sung. Awkward about speaking of their own loss, they are even less able to discuss mother's.

"You must come for Christmas" means "I love you," and "Hey, Mom, anytime you want to get yourself a boyfriend, it's OK with us" means "I know how lonely you are."

> *Right from the time of their father's death the children are going through private grief and their separation from a parent.*

Who Takes Care of Whom?

Mother finds it difficult both to ask for help and to reject well-intentioned assistance she does not want. The normal relationship of parent to child is upset. Who is taking care of whom? With teenagers, the relationship sometimes doesn't change so much as stagnate. In most cases the children and mother pull together when the father has died and are able to become a very close family. When mother works, everyone pitches in. But often we hear of the adolescent boy or girl who "won't talk about it." The reasons are varied—fear of death, guilt about having been at fault, guilt about not feeling strong remorse, and of course, fear of emotions.

> *Talk about Dad naturally and reminisce as you wish.*

There are probably others too; adolescents are exquisitely tuned. Sometimes family counseling helps—it's worth trying. But what widowed mothers say helped most was patience; not giving in to the temptation to react in kind. Talk about Dad naturally and reminisce as you wish. Eventually your child may respond and you can share your feelings with each other.

Not everyone has children; such couples are disparagingly called *childless*. Too often women are made to feel that widowhood would be less painful had they had children. One of the first questions widows ask each other on first meeting is, "Do you have children?" Then "How many?" and "Where do they live?"—as though their blessings can be counted by those answers.

Paradoxically, the general conversation then somehow evolves from family constellation to family grievances: how children never phone, about a daughter who is always running around somewhere in Europe and a son who owns a racehorse and, Lord help me, is getting married for the fourth time.

Certainly, children are the insurance we cash in when there is a crisis in our lives, but as the lady said, "They have their own lives to live." There are no studies to show that widows with children make a better adjustment. If you have children you will probably find them an important link in the transition you are going through, but not the only one. If you do not have children, other links will grow stronger; but like all widows, you'll find wholeness is up to you.

Your Parents

If they are both still alive, your parents become the family worriers. Just as you were beginning to keep a watchful eye out for them, they shift into reverse and try to reassume their parent role. A more likely possibility is that you, the widowed daughter, have a widowed mother and are saying, "I never realized what she had to cope with when my father died." Then, out of a sense of guilt, you feel you should make up for having been so insensitive. Mother comes to visit. Next, the family sees the consolidation of the two households as a sensible arrangement. "After all," sister says, "mother is getting on and the two of you can keep each other company."

Not being maneuvered into that situation may take more skill than that needed by a bullfighter in the ring, but it is worth the fight. In that particular scenario the losses usually outweigh the gains. Mother leaves her friends and community behind, and daughter forgoes the necessary and difficult push ahead of making new friends and changes because mother is there.

His Parents

They, or his widowed mother and all the sisters and the brothers on his side of the family, have suffered a loss in their family unit. They and the widow experience this in different ways. Their memories take precedence in time over the widow's. Mother has lost her son, the sisters and brothers their brother, and the widow her husband. But the absence of their disputed territory doesn't always bring them closer. Demanding mothers-in-law can become, out of panic, more demanding. A competitive sister-in-law becomes more gloating. When younger children are involved, the widow, as the crucial kingpin, has additional responsibilities to consider. (See Young Widows.)

Sisters and Brothers

What happens here? Thinking you may now be closer to the sister, eight years older and with whom you never had much in common, you visit her with high hopes for improving the relationship.

As one woman put it, "I spent two weeks in Kansas City looking for the sister I never had, in the city I never liked, and I felt I was in the wrong all the time. I must have been crazy." (Wouldn't it be ideal if everyone had a storybook sister?)

Your brother, never very affectionate or close, takes over, uninvited, as financial adviser. Or, worse, he and his wife are so worried that you will seek their financial help that they haven't called since the funeral. Like the sister relationship, the ties you have with brothers will not necessarily revert overnight to fill the gap in your life, even if their disapproval of your husband caused a gap in the first place. You may be longing for an altered relationship, but your brother may not know what you are talking about.

Family Dilemmas

Here are some other most-often-expressed family dilemmas, perhaps not in your marching order, but easily recognized nevertheless.

PROBLEM ONE: Your husband was "the good guy:" He indulged the children, was at his mother's beck and call for changing light bulbs, and the champion yes-sayer. Now you are caught in the trap of following his lead or giving out a few loud, healthy no's, something you'd wanted to do for more than 25 years. Initially after his death, everyone was careful not to change the expected patterns. You felt resentful about inheriting that trait of your husband, but felt obliged to act as he would have. Now what?

PROBLEM TWO: Your husband was the decision-maker. You deferred because you thought he knew better and you didn't know. Now everyone zooms into the vacuum to give you advice and help. Your in-laws move

You may be longing for an altered relationship, but your brother or sister may not know what you are talking about.

their RV into your driveway for January "to keep you company." Your mother comes to visit for February and March because the family thinks you'll both be happier because you are now two widows alone. The local son and family cheer you up by coming for Sunday dinner every week and filling in your other time with a bit of babysitting. Now, if you change this scenario by discovering you have emerging opinions and a desire for occasional privacy, the rippling effect throughout the family is horrendous.

Be on notice that the difficult period is yet to come: the time when you are feeling more independent and confident. That change takes place slowly—unnoticed and unmarked. We find out that hands-off comes about less easily than hands-on. It's hard to change the scene.

I can remember my cousin Hal calling me from New Jersey and sending me special-delivery packets about financial investments after my husband died. He freely gave advice and comfort. In my confused, ignorant state I gratefully clung to his every word. He was my brother, my mentor and my rescuer. My need was his need, but once I outgrew my student status, his pride in me was edged with regret. Gradually we became cousins again.

> *The difficult period is yet to come: the time when you are feeling more independent and confident.*

My own son, who takes delight in my busy and active life, can often be heard to say, with an edge of pique in his voice, "We tried calling you all weekend." I dare say that those who have made the transition from Here to There have heard that remark a few hundred times and realize with surprise each time that you are no longer so needy. Perhaps you even feel a little guilty at having tipped the independency scale in your favor.

All this may sound negative. Your experiences with your family may be ideal, better than ever. Your soap opera may not appear in the stories above. But I have rarely met a widow who, in honest reflection, has not laughed or cried over a family situation that resulted from her changed family position. Human behavior is affected by human behavior.

The comforting thought, though, is that one person does have the power to affect solutions. But the law is tough, for it says:

THE PERSON WHO WANTS THE CHANGE
HAS TO BE THE PERSON TO MAKE THE CHANGE.

I used to have that sign in my counseling office; some people would take one look and hate it on the spot. It seems unfair when we are convinced it is the other person who needs to change. You can't will change, nor can you make much happen with wishes.

Determining what you really want and being responsible for taking the very first step is the key to a smoother working family. For example: You don't care to be the constant last-minute baby-sitter. You can say that you love being with the children but now that you are beginning to expand your activities you will happily give them two Saturday nights a month. Period! You don't sulk, feel resentful or wish they wouldn't ask. You clarify in your own head what you want—in this case not to be imposed upon—and you make the change with some give-and-take.

To the daughter who still can't make ends meet and calls frequently for extra cash you say, "I know you depended on Daddy and miss him. We both do, but now we must both learn how to manage on our own. I can help you with *x* dollars a year but the rest is up to you." And remember, no guilt.

To the son who took total control of your affairs at the beginning and is still saving you worry and enlightenment, you gently remind him that the time has come for you to learn.

To the mother-in-law who calls on you to change light bulbs and do other inherited jobs, you tell her you're going to send over your handyman. If you don't have one, run right out and get one.

When "poor me" hasn't had a phone call from whoever it is that never calls, *you* pick up the phone and call. Do you

Determining what you really want and being responsible for taking the very first step is the key to a smoother working family.

want to be the one who waits or the one who acts?

And to yourself, you say, "I am the hub, the axis of the family, and it must be right for me, otherwise nothing works." Sometimes your action alone will be effective. Other times, you may negotiate and work out a compromise. Still other times you will have to circle your wants and set them aside, for action on another day.

Nothing is forever. Your life is changing.

When "poor me" hasn't had a phone call from whoever it is that never calls, you pick up the phone and call.

Widowhood and the Calendar

WHILE MOST OF US, in our grief, cannot retain a fact, a number or a face for more than five minutes, our heads are crammed with significant dates we cannot forget. At first, like an alcoholic counting days of sobriety, we tick off the time since he died in weeks and months.

Ask a recent widow "How long?" and you get the answer to the hour. Fortunately, as our brain cells return to some of their former memory functions, we dispense with the daily count. Rarely are we able to obliterate the birthday, the wedding anniversary or special events that meant so much to the two of us, however. They remain on our mind's calendar.

During the first year of widowhood, passing through that calendar is more frightening in anticipation than in actuality. We have all read newspaper and magazine articles warning about the disasters, the severe depression, the suicides to which surviving spouses are prone, on what has come to be called *the anniversary date*. What seems to occur more often is that the anxiety concerning those dreaded dates looms larger than the actual experience.

Special Dates

Widows, in reporting how they survived one of their special days, say the days prior to the actual date were more difficult. That feeling of apprehension was vividly described by one widow when she said, "I dreaded June 25th. We would have been married 25 years, and I fully expected something terrible—I didn't know what—to happen. I think I was afraid I would go crazy. All week I felt terribly depressed, but when the 25th came I actually felt relieved. Isn't that weird?"

No. Special occasions—birthdays, wedding anniversary, and the romantic Valentine's Day—are not easily thrown away like yesterday's garbage. They are dates to be reckoned with. Most of us acknowledge that we are sad, mad and depressed and feel very sorry for ourselves at such times—perhaps for a whole week before the actual date. But we also count it as a milestone when we survive that day for the first time. The second time around is less foreboding.

But we also count it as a milestone when we survive that day for the first time. The second time around is less foreboding.

The birthdays of famous people long dead are celebrated, but not the birthday of a dead spouse; it is not standard procedure. Likewise, the wedding-anniversary date. With friends and family we are carefully shy: We spare each other with silence. One mother of seven children, all scattered about the country, reported that each one of them phoned during the week of their father's birthday "just to say hello," without mentioning the occasion.

My own husband died on October 31st, and—would you believe it?—for many years good and dear friends would call to ask casually what I was doing for Halloween. At the time I refrained from upsetting their equilibrium by answering flippantly, "Oh, the usual trick-or-treating," or from thanking them appreciatively—as I really wanted to—for remembering my loss. Now, after sharing widowhood with many hundreds of other widows, I would. Unspoken words—lost opportunities.

That applies also to those new special occasions and family gatherings where *his* absence is on everyone's mind, but mention of *him* is carefully avoided. A woman illustrated that point with her poignant account of her grandson's confirmation celebration. "I felt so sad because Arthur wasn't there. He would have loved it. Finally, I couldn't stand it, and I said to my son at dinner, 'Your father would have been so proud today.' My son looked at me for a minute, stood up, lifted his wineglass and announced, 'To my father, who is with us all today.' Everyone toasted, and Arthur *was* there with his family. I really felt good. We all did."

If his birthday is difficult, our own can be worse. Going out to dinner with another widow, feasting on a birthday cake made by a granddaughter or going off to the woods to meditate will never replace that early-morning happy-birthday kiss and the blouse that had to be returned for the correct size.

Try a Little Self-Indulgence

Some women resort to buying their own special-occasion presents and find that a pretty good solution. "I wanted a new camera," one widow explained, "but couldn't justify the expense to myself until I thought that Harvey would have asked me what I wanted for my birthday and that I would have told him, as I always did. So I said, 'Happy Birthday' to myself and bought it." (That's how I got my stereo system.)

A little bit of self-indulgence can also turn a poor-me day into a rather manageable Valentine's Day. For reasons only Madison Avenue can answer, Valentine's Day has come to mean that all the world has a lover. And more widows fall apart on that day than 16-year-olds. A tactic that works surprisingly well is to buy yourself something frivolous if that date has meaning for you: flowers, a new pair of earrings, or if absolutely desperate, candy.

You can think of it therapeutically: You're not rewarding self-pity, but preventing it.

The exact opposite, however, turning outward, works equally well for those who send cards and greetings to others and become more involved in adding to other people's happiness. "Bake a heart-shaped cake for some neighbor kids," one widow suggested, "and stop feeling sorry for yourself. Valentine's Day, big deal."

Widowers don't seem to have as much trouble with significant dates as do widows. Probably because they never remembered all of them in the first place or because significant occasions and dates are more meaningful to women. One widow

You can think of it therapeutically: You're not rewarding self-pity, but preventing it.

momentarily confused her birthday with her anniversary when she was talking to her daughter on the phone and quickly added, "In a way I was *born* on my wedding day." For her, the date was still honored. New widowers, on the other hand, falter over wedding anniversaries and seasonal holidays at the beginning, but the dates in themselves are less important and they are fewer. "Valentine's Day," as the lady said, is "no big deal."

Difficult as it is to imagine, those anniversary dates that at first cause the widow—and widower—such apprehension fade with the years. No one need feel disloyal when some milestone passes quietly unnoticed until a week later. There are new dates to remember. My remarkable daughter-in-law held on to my second grandchild for two extra weeks so that May 15th became Peter's birthday and no longer my wedding anniversary. That was indeed a double gift to me and not easily replicated. Nonetheless, there are new dates in everyone's fortune cookie.

The point of all this is that significant dates need not be feared, forgotten or silently endured. For as long as you want, acknowledge the day, celebrate if you wish. Remember out loud with those who also remember, and put it aside when you are ready.

Divorced, Widowed—
Is It the Same?

DIVORCEES, WIDOWS—we are *not* the same, new widows contend. Divorcees may know of rejection, guilt, anger and low morale, but they do not know our irrevocable loss. No, we are *not* the same. Still, we are always being addressed as one under such titles as SINGLE AGAIN and WOMEN ALONE. Widows wonder why they feel pushed out of shape by the inclusion. We read all the motivational books and magazine articles that are supposed to inspire us all to join, to do and to let go. But we don't give a damn and can't agree with the comparison, say widows.

Support groups that attempt to incorporate both recent divorcees and recent widows into the same support system are often warlike and seldom productive. Divorcees and widows view their past and future from opposite positions. The former regards tomorrow as a demand; the latter, as a reproach; one sees white, the other sees black.

Newly divorced women say they understand the widow's loss. The unwillingly divorced woman might say to the widow, "You're luckier, I was dumped" and even the extreme, "Given the choice, I would rather see the bastard dead." Despite the lack of malice intended, these statements offer no great comfort to the widow who feels she would do anything to have him alive. "I can't relate to a person like that," she says. End of group.

True, not all newly divorced women feel liberated and not all new widows are left desolate, but support groups—not to mention generalities—are not made up of exceptions. It's fair to say that while most divorcees do not consider themselves so different from widows, most widows do not abide the comparison. At least that was my conclusion after three dismal attempts at integrating all the Single Agains into one group.

It's fair to say that while most divorcees do not consider themselves so different from widows, most widows do not abide the comparison.

Because the issue is not whether it is better to have loved and lost, but what you perceive as having lost. For divorcees the best of times are hardly remembered; the worst of times are in sharper focus. Ask a divorcee what her marriage was like, and she will surely not begin with "We were a very close couple." The best of times have receded into a tangle of unhappiness. I once heard a woman, long divorced and remarried, say of her first husband, "John died last week, and ever since my mind has been flooded with good memories. I had completely forgotten the great barbecues he did and what fun they were for the kids—and for all of us."

Different Attitudes

Newly divorced women also have quite a different attitude about dating and marriage. They have more ego involvement, a greater need to look to the opposite sex for approval and proof of worth— or justification. A recent widow, on the other hand, has lost a battle with death, not with another woman. Usually, she has no immediate need to prove herself sexually. Nor is a new wardrobe, cosmetic surgery, dieting or a new image at the top of the list for her right then.

Divorced women complain because their friends, like their possessions, are divided. Some go to him and some to her. Widows say after the first hello they are all good-byes; their coupled friends fall away completely. The divorced say they have less financial security; the widowed say they are poorer with no recourse through the courts. The widow sees the divorcee as having contributed to her own situation—to a greater or lesser degree as the case may be— while she is a total victim. Further, where divorcees have a sense of failure and blame themselves for some flaw in their own character, widows also fault themselves for not being able to stand up against the forces of destiny. That's in addition to the many more "if onlys" and "I should haves."

Another interesting difference comes in the way divorcees and widows view living alone. A divorced woman once told me that she got down on her knees every night and prayed she wouldn't wake up in the morning from a dream and find her husband in bed next to her. I'd heard so many widows say, in almost the same words, the exact opposite; it was like a cold shower of dawning. Further, the average divorcee makes a different kind of adjustment in her environment, her home; she opts for changes. You can bet you're not going to see pictures of her recently departed spouse in view or his favorite chair. She will not dwell on composing a scrapbook of their happy hours together, she will not devotedly complete a project that he started, or maintain any more continuity with her past wife-role than is absolutely necessary.

Choice versus No Choice

Well, that's not what a widow does. Divorcees and widows part with their men in quite different ways. On closer examination, though, we see that while the comparisons have some validity, the gulf between divorcees and widows is triggered by the one element not shared: Choice. In every divorce at least one person had that luxury.

Often I hear a widow berate herself because she unexpectedly feels out of tune with a divorced friend or family member. "I should be grateful to have her company, but I can't really talk to her. What's wrong with me?" she'll ask. Maybe the answer is that, until it happens to us, we just don't know any better.

The gap exists at the beginning; we take different passageways. But in time—yes, time—most of us have single friends that come from both sides of the marriage track. You'll hardly notice and it will hardly matter after a while.

It's a lucky thing, too, because we SINGLE AGAIN and WOMEN ALONE people need all the friends we can get.

Speak Up, I Can't Hear You

IF YOU SEE TWO WOMEN in a restaurant firmly refusing a table close to the back kitchen door while pointing to the nice little booth up front, you might think they either were born that way or are mid-term into an assertiveness-training class. Look more closely! Chances are they are widows who, after dealing with lawyers, bankers and bureaucrats, realized that silence is not golden and the little wheel that does not squeak also does not move.

Generally, men are more assertive than women. Moreover, the early division of labor rules established for many women dictated that men spoke up and women pulled at their sleeve and told them not to get too excited. But even today's woman, including those married women who handle many of the couple's joint affairs confidently and competently during the marriage, say that without the backup of the male figure they feel intimidated by the system, vulnerable and slightly paranoid.

What most widows learn, by experience, trial and error, is that we can take care of ourselves once we learn to speak up clearly, appropriately and with authority. Cheer up, it only takes a year. Perhaps two years if you cry easily or assume, as I did, that because your husband treated you like an intelligent, capable woman others would too. Or that logic and reason prevail on a day-to-day basis.

> *We can take care of ourselves once we learn to speak up clearly, appropriately and with authority.*

You should know right at the outset that in some ways there is, indeed, a plot against you: Nothing will go right. If you patiently stand in line, it is the wrong line. Staying too long "on hold" will net you a disconnect; standing by obediently for that "I'll call you right back" call will give you fallen arches. Room numbers are not always consecutive in governmental buildings. And if you make a right you should have gone left.

To survive without the male voice of authority—or at least the voice that helped you laugh at the absurd—you must become cunningly effective. Seldom does the "poor little widow" routine work more than once with the same person. You must learn a whole new vocabulary. No more weasel words, now you concentrate on command words—polite, but definite. You turn "Would it be possible for Mr. Jones to let me know?" into "Please have Mr. Jones call me this morning. This is important." Throw out the humble "Can you let me" and "I don't understand why" and shoot dead center with "This is in regard to . . . please send" (or "connect me with . . .")—whatever the appropriate action verb of choice. Notice use of the word *action*.

> *No more weasel words, now you concentrate on command words— polite, but definite.*

Use Command Words

Use command words when dealing with the telephone dragons who guard the castle so closely you can never talk to "the boss." Doctors must have a special source—picture dragon person saying to the boss, "Jane Wooman wishes to talk to you" rather than "That pesky Mrs. Wooman is on the phone again." Select your words accordingly and notice use of first the name rather than Mrs. So and So; an executive strategy. You field the usual useless request to state your reason and purpose by saying, quietly and firmly, "Just give Mr. Boss my name." I can't tell you why that works oftener than it doesn't; maybe if you think you are important, others do, too.

Use the Telephone

Widows cut their eyeteeth on Social Security, license and tax bureaus, utility companies and what seems an endless parade of officialdom. For dealing with the superstructure of bureaucracy it's best to use the telephone as much as possible. State your information in a firm voice with simple, concise sentences. Leave out all extraneous information that might confuse a 10-year-old, such as how long you were married, your degree of happiness and your state of mind. At the beginning of the conversation, determine if you are speaking to the right person and make note of his or her name—use the name at least once in conversation. If you have questions, start out by saying something like, "I have three questions regarding . . . " and count to make sure all are answered.

Positive and Businesslike

Don't ramble or engage in unnecessary chatter; sound positive and businesslike. When you are thwarted by negatives such as "Those are the rules," "That's not my department," or "He's not at his desk," ask to speak to a person in charge or get that person's name and call him back. See yourself as an executive, talk to people at the top when possible, and make executive statements: "Thank you Mr. Mann, then you'll be personally responsible for taking care of that for me." (That's one that should be written next to the phone until you get used to saying it convincingly.) Write all the facts in your log and should Mr. Mann not follow through, call him back and remind him.

Most of the tearful complaints heard from widows concern the professionals who handle estate and probate matters. The widow has a million questions. The lawyer is difficult to reach, the accountant is talking in a language that whistles through her head, and the doctor's office keeps sending the same bill in spite of the previous discussion. Sometimes these are the very people we—and our husbands—thought would be our source of help. Frequently they are, but they also may be the most difficult because it is particularly awkward to pester or question the work of an "old buddy" by discussing money or his judgment. Sadly we discover that a straightforward approach would have been wiser, as this widow learned: "I called him whenever I had a problem; he was my husband's lawyer for 17 years. 'Call me anytime,' he said. You should have seen the bill. That son of a gun clocked all those calls and charged me by the minute when I asked him for the name of his plumber." Of course, you don't call your lawyer for a plumber, but if you do, better ask for costs in advance.

Pin It Down

For any transaction—big, small, friendly or impersonal—ask, "How much?" and "When?" If the work is computed on an hourly basis, request "a ballpark figure." Try not to put yourself in the wait-forever position; get a date either when you may again inquire or when you may expect the matter to be concluded. That way your papers have a better chance of not getting shuffled to the bottom of the pile. Be polite but firm even when it's your father's brother.

One of the most common complaints about lawyers is the dreadfully long time it takes them to conclude the legal details. True, the courts move slowly when probate is involved, but lawyers, as well as other professionals, think they are being compassionate and sympathetic when they say, "No hurry, we'll take care of this later." They're giving you time for that supposed recovery. And, of course, the very opposite may be true. One widow observed: "I guess probate and some of the other legal affairs were all mileposts I had to pass, but each time I had to write a check for the estate there was a jab. When I had to send for another copy of the death certificate I dreaded getting the mail. It went on for 19 months; no one was in a hurry. And I was too meek to say anything." I guess we have to undertake the education of attorneys, accountants and the hopeless IRS; widows can't look ahead when they have to keep looking back.

> *One of the most common complaints about lawyers is the dreadfully long time it takes them to conclude the legal details.*

Why Assertiveness Is Important

Shyness, fear of sounding stupid, hurting feelings, provoking anger and the inability to think of the right words are some of the reasons given for keeping silent, or saying "yes" when you mean "no." While the unaccustomed demands experienced during the first year of widowhood are enough to make the most sure-footed woman feel inadequate, many women are looking at an old problem. They have been "good girls" and dutiful wives with uninterrupted continuity.

Left now to manage on their own there are three choices: become dependent on someone else, continue to compromise their rights— or change.

In your case you may not even realize that a change—we won't even consider the first two options—is possible because you have become so accustomed to your particular brand of suffering. Women tell how the light bulb came on when they heard others standing up for their rights, respect and needs. Inspired and encouraged, they find they can, with practice, say "no." After a few dress rehearsals, they can make positive statements. In most communities courses in assertiveness training are available. The course probably will not transform you into the Queen of England, but you will have some moments when you *feel* like the Queen of England.

What I learned in the assertiveness-training course I took was to say "no" without feeling obliged to add "but" or "because." I learned to say "that's not the issue" when someone was trying to pressure me with extraneous, guilt-provoking arguments. In case you also never did so before, go ahead and try it. Say "no thanks" without apologizing.

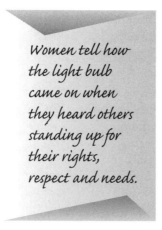

Women tell how the light bulb came on when they heard others standing up for their rights, respect and needs.

Is Assertiveness Training for You?

If you're wondering how to tell whether you can benefit from a course in assertiveness, the flat answer is: Everyone can—the meek and the bold. Obviously, assertive and aggressive are not the same. The overbearing, rude person has as much to overcome as the shrinking violet. She may not always identify herself as such. Most people recognize their own blocks, but if you need a gauge, see how you score on these questions.

Do you:

- Never take "no" for an answer?
- Feel you always have to fight for your rights?
- Easily lose your temper, speak loudly and regret it later?
- Feel righteously hostile and leave no friends in your wake?

If you answer "yes" to all of these questions, sign up; you need modifying and developing better skills of diplomacy. If you answer "no" to these questions, continue.

Can you:

- Refuse to lend a friend money?
- Ask for the return of something borrowed (including money)?
- Resist buying when the clerk has taken a long time with you?
- Say "no" without an explanation?
- Say "no" if you think people will not like you?
- Tell someone when they have hurt your feelings?
- Disagree with a person who sounds authoritative?
- Send back food in a restaurant when you should?
- Take criticism?
- Express your own opinion with no apology?
- Receive compliments?
- Start a conversation with strangers?

If you answer "yes" to all of these questions, take the course anyway. It will probably be worthwhile, usually fun and short-term. Find out about these courses from your local community college or community center.

At this very moment you can also start looking at yourself more objectively, at your submerged blocks and unspoken goals. Stand in front of the mirror and tell yourself loudly and clearly what it is *you* want.

The art of assertiveness starts with clarifying your right to be a person. It emphasizes what you may have forgotten, that you may speak out and you may chase any dream you've a mind to. You can learn to make "I" statements instead of trying to manipulate other people—and yourself—with guilt or pity.

Try it out now, away from the mirror, for real. Begin some of those "Would it be possible . . ." "Whatever you think . . ." sentences with "I want . . .", "I like . . ." Go around for a day being direct, politely honest and convinced that no one can read your mind any more than you can read theirs. You'll see the world unfold before you!

Practice Makes Perfect

One standard technique in assertion training is the practice exercise, in which you role-play in the classroom or deliberately create uncomfortable situations for yourself outside the class. You might be asked to do something cheeky, like buy a gallon of gasoline with a $20 bill or place yourself in any other situation that makes you squirm. You look at the outer limits you have assigned to yourself and decide whether you want to expand those limits as well as how to do so. For the most part, the thrust of the exercises is to make you feel better about yourself because you are more effective. You can try that on your own just for the heck of it.

The thrust of the exercises is to make you feel better about yourself because you are more effective.

For my assignment, I had to ask the waiter in a busy restaurant to divide the check three ways and to charge the amounts separately to my credit card and those of my two companions. To our surprise the waiter didn't mind. Later, when we asked him why, he said his men customers frequently made that request.

As it turns out, one person's assertion is another person's birthright.

Take pen and legal pad in hand and note the people and situations that cause fluttering stomach butterflies. Do you avoid resolving problem areas, and does that as a result affect your lifestyle and relationships? It's understood that there are times when you grin and bear it. We all know people with whom the better part of assertion is to say "You may be right" or "There you go"—both of which can be almost satisfying to either side.

But the majority of widows will come up with a list that will easily yield to a new approach. None of us ever reaches the point of perfection where the right words slide off the tongue at the exact moment we need them rather than in the middle of the next night. Even then all is not lost; it's always possible to go back and try again rather than ruminate over past history.

> *A good way to clarify responsibility is to ask yourself, "Whose problem is it?"*

We are forever taking on other people's problems and then feeling put upon because we have made ourselves part of the solution. A good way to clarify responsibility is to ask yourself, "Whose problem is it?" Even a sticky dilemma—lending money to the children or being asked to baby-sit on the very weekend you thought you might join a friend for fishing—lends itself to this kind of analysis.

One woman struggled over whether to pay a roofer more than the originally agreed-upon contract price when he claimed he had erred in his original addition. Was that his problem or her problem? Should the decision to pay the revised amount be based on how she viewed his work or on her guilt? Would her husband have been presented with the same set of facts? That may not be your average situation, but it's a rather classic dilemma in comparable situations. About the best one can do is assess the situation fairly. Should the problem clearly not be of your making you'll find it easy to respond accordingly. "I'm sorry, Mr. Roofer, that is what I budgeted" or, "Let's split the difference," or meekly pay up. As for the children, you tell them you can baby-sit next week, you've already made other plans for this weekend; or simply state you don't have the money to lend them at this time. When you oblige, do it because you want to, not because you are afraid to refuse.

If your sweet smile and nodding agreement is a façade, a cover-up, and at core you are afraid to displease or incur anger, you must get used to the idea that everyone is not always going to love you. After all, you don't love everyone either. So keep a few sentences ready until you reach the stage where you can speak up and express yourself as you would like: "Let me think about that," "I don't agree with you completely," or "Thank you, let me check the date. I'll let you know."

Speaking up is merely a form of expressing what's on your mind. If you're feeling indecisive, let others know. Not only are you honestly communicating, you're preserving your rights. In time, you won't feel so indecisive. You'll have developed the strength and conviction to speak your mind.

Speaking up is merely a form of expressing what's on your mind.

Dating

DATING! Widows over the age of 50 giggle when they hear the word applied to themselves.

"This man has to be 65 if he's a day," an attractive sixtyish woman was recounting, "and he asks me, not if I'd like to go out with him, but if I'm interested in dating. It sounded so ridiculously juvenile, I couldn't keep a straight face."

Three months later that widow was dating, but she preferred to describe it as *seeing somebody*. She thought it sounded more mature. Not that there is so much difference among the words. The big difference is in the social change that has taken place within our adult lives. Widows used to look to chance and their own little social network as ways to meet eligible husbands. Today, not only have the networks been greatly expanded, we have also gone from "eligible husbands" to "partners." Dating, whatever your semantic preference and no matter what your age, still means boy meets girl, and when boy meets girl, one or the other may have marriage in mind.

When the "boy" is a widower he definitely is more marriage-minded because the great majority of older men are married—and that includes remarriages—compared with women of like ages. Further, U.S. Census figures show widowers remarry within three years and widows within five. Reliable observers say the waiting period for men has been rapidly shortening and men now customarily remarry within a year. The underlying reason for all those statistics is neatly stated by retirement-community residents from Florida to California when they quote, "Around here, when a man dies we all send cards; when a woman dies we all bring casseroles."

And that, really, goes to the heart of the matter, or two hearts, strictly speaking. Women, as we keep noting, far outnumber men and are consequently more available. So they find they have to be more forthright if they want to date. While you can surely forgo the casserole, you should know your own mind. Then, whether you actively stalk or passively survey depends on your style and inclination.

Time-worn fantasies such as running into an old high-school flame at a class reunion or meeting a man on a cruise are stories that are passed around like Christmas fruitcakes by well-meaning friends and family who see remarriage as the only happy ending. Instead of feeling encouraged, the widow who is still trying to find her own direction may end up feeling like a deficient sorority girl without a Saturday-night date.

You may not be the least bit interested in a male relationship. Your life may be filled with women friends, couples, family and outside interests; a man is just what you *don't* want. You don't *need* a man. So don't allow yourself to feel pressured to join the parade if you are following your heart. But also don't reject the idea because of guilt or fear. Anyone who has had an intimate relationship of long standing feels shy and insecure about the unknown. So, you really have to be honest with yourself as to your ultimate desire and clear it with yourself. As for guilt: Be guilty only if it makes you feel better.

The Waiting Period

The respectable waiting period of a year is still traditionally observed. But many widows say it took them much longer before they had any interest in, or could even contemplate, male companionship. However, it is not at all unusual, sinful or untimely for a widow to seek male companionship earlier. She would be crazy, though, to get married while still grieving or simply because she is afraid to be alone. "Better to make a mistake than marry one," said a widow who discovered after a whirlwind courtship that she had bartered security

One woman says, "I could never go back to being a housekeeper and there aren't many men who can accept that."

for an alcoholic.

What each woman has to decide for herself is whether it is worth it. *No vale la pena* ("It's not worth the pain") is an old Spanish adage and also the adage of many widows who shun the dating scene. One woman says, "I could never go back to being a housekeeper and there aren't many men who can accept that." Another, talking about the couples in her mobile-home park says, "I don't envy the women who have remarried. They think they're getting companionship, but what they get is an old man." That's a rather sweeping generalization, but it does take note of the ever-increasing age disparity between men and women in second and third marriages. One hardly blinks anymore when an 80-year-old man marries a woman 20 years his junior. At any rate, there are women who say they enjoy their independence and are not interested in giving it up, women who are not interested in a man at any price. Other women say, "Only if someone very special comes along."

> *Other women say, "Only if someone very special comes along."*

These women may be considered *nonserious daters,* and they convey their message both by their demeanor and in interactions with men. Men claim they can tell when a woman is "not interested."

Other widows, called *serious daters,* may be right out there "looking for a man" or "giving out vibes"—however you describe it—with ease. Still others would like to, but dislike the image they might project; while others are ever hopeful that Santa Claus will intervene. Sure, that happens, but to everyone else, not you. When dreams of romance float through your head, you might as well explore your reality and give it a try.

Meeting an Eligible Man

The most comfortable way to meet an eligible man is through a friend. While a single man is the greater dinner-party prize, you may also net invitations if you let your friends and family know that you are ready to date. Discourage them from secret plots and premature meetings, however. Good friends, a couple, once invited me to their golf club for dinner and rounded out the table with three eligible men—there are a lot of widowers at golf clubs. As soon as I realized what they were plotting, I developed the only allergy I've ever had in my life; my eyes began to run, nasal passages closed, and whatever words I spoke came through double tissues. To this day I don't know whether I was reacting to panic or disinterest, but I can tell you that none of the men were tempted to find out. Nothing will dampen the conviviality of a group seated around a table faster than Typhoid Mary coming down with a cold.

Simultaneous with telling your friends, you had better also talk over with your family the fact that you want to start dating. Get what you hope will be their blessings, but most of all avoid acting furtive and feeling guilty. You won't like it. One woman told me every time her "gentleman friend" came to the house she removed the photograph of her husband that sat on a table in the living room, replacing it when the children came over. I imagine this kept her as busy as the soprano in a comic opera.

The next best social-meeting opportunities are to be found with the many groups for singles at churches, community and sports clubs and similar organizations. Everyone is there for the same reason: to meet people with similar interests. The female boosters of singles clubs report that they meet more interesting women than men, but that's fine too. No matter where you go it seems women outnumber men. I once took a fly-fishing class and a woman on entering the room and seeing that half the class was female groaned, "I thought I would be the only woman here."

There are a growing number of by-invitation-only singles groups for older people that you will hear about when you travel the circuit. Some advertise their services, others are known by word of mouth. Singles groups that cater to younger people may also be selective and not admit as many women as apply. Don't feel offended; it's not you, it's the law of supply and demand at work. A fortyish attorney who joined a group that was limited to professionals under 50 said that after the first year only the women were held to those criteria. Although she was planning soon to marry a 58-year-old auto salesman she had met through the group, the inequity still bothered her.

If you like dancing, some of the older hotels in large cities have revived the tea-dancing custom, where it is quite proper for unaccompanied ladies to join gentlemen for a dance or two. At worst, you will have heard some pleasant music and have had enjoyed a good cup of tea. Square-dancing groups, which once accepted only couples, are now welcoming single women and no longer frown on the old European custom of women dancing with women.

"Personal" ads have become a popular approach. We hear the same old story—an older man's ad will attract ten times more answers than an older woman's (one man told me he received more than 100 answers to his inquiry for meeting an interesting mature woman). You may find an amusing correspondent through that approach. Your children will have a fit, though, and worry about your safety.

And finally, there are the age-old diversions—cruises, classes and card groups that cater to your particular peer group, interests and nonmarried status. But, and here is the key point, don't be dismayed by those with unbridled determination. To give you an idea, once at an Elderhostel I observed one woman snatch the roster of names immediately on arrival, mark off the uncoupled male names, and then seat herself next to one of them whenever possible. The rest of us poor, ignorant souls studied Greek mythology.

Best Place to Meet a Man

Someone was saying she had heard that the best place to meet a man is at the supermarket around 6 p.m. when the singles are homeward bound. "That's fine," she added, "but what time do the retired gentlemen shop?" Probably at the same hour, because the differences between old and young men and women are growing slimmer.

Young widows have much the same reentry problems as older widows: They are just as reluctant to expose themselves to risk and rejection. I'm not sure about supermarket meetings, but no one need resort to singles bars or go on the prowl; there are more dignified opportunities, as you will discover as you investigate and talk to other women who are also socially active. And please do investigate. Most women are reasonably cautious and not dumb enough to walk off with a stranger they met at a bar. It's also not a good idea to invite a man into your house for a cup of coffee—even after a church social—if you don't know anything about him. At worst, he may consider that an invitation for more than you intended. Next worst, you may need a steam shovel to get rid of him. Until you know the man and have met before in public places or among groups, invite another couple when you ask him over for dinner the first time.

Meeting Is Just the First Step

Meeting a man is only the beginning, as you can see, and no wonder some women cringe at the thought. They too easily recall their adolescent embarrassments and the terror social events held for them. "I'll never go through that again; it was bad enough then, but it's a meat market out there now," they say. The women who have been happily dating claim that to be a misconception. "Men are just as worried," they say, and point out that maturity brings the advantage of social sense and experience. After the first five minutes, talking to a man is just talking to a man, and the rest is like riding a bicycle: You don't forget.

The very dedicated man pursuer may scare off more partners than she snatches, so if you are yourself you will like yourself and enjoy yourself—and even learn all about Greek mythology. Contrary to what you hear, dating does not have to include sex unless and until you wish to become an equal partner. The man who thinks otherwise will inform you of his agenda early, and you can explain yours.

All this may sound complicated and perhaps foreboding, but the basic ABC's of dating are relatively unchanged since you were a teenager, if that's what you are worried about. As a single woman you have many options; our society allows you freedom to choose and to behave according to your own morality and self-interest. Women are bolder than they used to be, men say; women are more honest, women say.

Sex

I SUSPECT THAT EVERY SIX MINUTES somewhere around the world a widow is saying, "I don't care about remarrying. I would just like to go out to dinner with a man once in a while." The widow's refrain!

That litany represents for many widows the extent of their sexual lust. They had a good marriage with gratifying (or not-so-gratifying) sex and really don't want to "take care of another man." Other widows are simply retrenching.

The ratio of men to women over age 50 is statistically dispassionate—something like one to five. When you include men in prison, confirmed misanthropes and homosexuals, you begin to understand that the real numbers give women about the same chance as winning the jackpot in a state lottery. There is plenty of sex out there, but the average widow, with limited sexual experiences in her background and a bit of drab and droop in her foreground, hesitates to compete. She still harbors her girlhood fantasy about the right man coming along.

Often he does. But until then, what does the widow do about her need to be touched, intimately involved and sexually stimulated? The choices are clearly limited. She can find a man, another woman, or enjoy her own company. And any of these choices may or may not include sex. It's an individual choice and more often than not, a private one. Whenever the subject of sex comes up in widow's support groups, someone usually chirps up, "And who remembers?" That brings nervous titters of laughter. For the most part the women are reluctant to initiate the subject. Once the floodgate is opened, however, everyone has a great deal that needs saying. Responses vary quite as much as you would expect, and nothing illustrates those variations as these two true anecdotes.

Two True Stories

First, the reaction of one lady in her early 70s listening to the group talk about whether it was sex they missed or just cuddling up to a warm body. "Well," she said, "you girls don't know how much all my friends envy me. Their husbands keep them up all night trying to come to climax, which they never do. They never get a night's sleep. Those men never give up."

In contrast, there was the National Conference for Widowed Persons Services that I attended at which sex was one of the program topics. The presenter, an associate professor who gave regular workshops on human sexuality, to her credit did not reshape her lecture for "little old ladies in tennis shoes." She spoke of options and choices for single women, covering celibacy, singles bars, living with a man, lesbian relationships and masturbation. The latter she elaborated on with a description and consumer mini-guide to vibrators. There was no need, she advised the audience, to go to a sex shop or buy an expensive device. "There is a very good regular vibrator put out by Hitachi for about $25." At that point a hand shot up, and a truly enthusiastic, grandmotherly looking woman, unable to wait for recognition, stood up to her full five feet. Here it comes, I thought, the morality lecture.

If the relationship is respectful and loving, inequities of education, social status, age and income are less important to them now.

The question asked, loud and clear, however, was "How do you spell *Hitachi?*"

There you have the full spectrum, from the widow who is grateful that she no longer has to bother, to the widow who is still curious and interested in exploring her sexual feelings. Be advised also that feelings can change. Most widows say they are disinterested in sex in early widowhood and then are surprised, pleased, or horrified—depending on their own code of ethics and individual guilt machine—when sexual desires reawaken.

Perhaps because they're willing to talk about it more freely, women in their 50s, more so than older widows—although there are no age limitations—report the absence of sex mostly to be a physiological problem. It is ironic that women at an age when they are reaching sexual maturity have such limited options. As one woman noted, "Just as I was no longer anxious about becoming pregnant or one of the kids popping into the room, and was really enjoying sex, it was all over." Some men, many women say, are only too ready to exploit the situation. The tales of decent and indecent propositions made to widows have come down through the ages.

When I first became widowed, I got as much advice—from both sexes—about lecherous men as I did about not doing anything for a year. And sure enough, one night at a dinner party, the man seated next to me put his hand on my knee, under the table, and whispered, "I pass your house all the time; anytime you'd like to share me with my wife, I'll be glad to stop by." This man was a leading citizen and, in addition, his wife was sitting right across the table, unaware, politely absorbed in conversation with a man who had his hands on his knife and fork. In spite of all the forewarnings, I was shocked. Typically, I didn't want to embarrass the pompous jerk or spoil the dinner party, so instead I placed his hand on the table, gave him a brittle smile and said, perhaps just a shade too loudly, "Sorry, I'm not very good at sharing."

It's my only contribution to the legends, but women tell me they receive offers from neighbors, husbands of good friends, and a variety of other unexpected outlets who believe that widows after a while are busting out of their britches. Widowers, too, have expressed an impressive collection of personal experiences that speak to the sexual aggressiveness of women as well.

Men and women have equal capacity for becoming involved in a relationship strictly for its sexual appeal. We hear about it from the families: about Dad who lost his head and behaved foolishly and Mom who lost her sense of reason and perhaps her bank account over a younger man. But children also become upset when their mothers, more so than their fathers, seek sexual gratification in an alliance they deem in any way unworthy of her. "He's a truck driver who never graduated from high school," a horrified son told me over the telephone one day. "My mother has a Ph.D. in chemistry, my father was a doctor." I didn't happen to know his mother, but widows—and indeed many women in their second and third marriages—will compromise one former value for a present-day one; it works out well enough. If the relationship is respectful and loving, inequities of education, social status, age and income are less important to them now.

Normal Is Whatever You Feel

The female libido is inexplicable. Some women postulate that the lack of sex is a greater hardship on them because they had good and fulfilling intimacies, but that certainly doesn't seem to be true for everyone. For many widows sex in the abstract has absolutely no appeal regardless of past experience. They turn off that particular switch for the time being, or forever. Contrarily, someone who had had terrible sex and had a "headache" for the past 20 years, suddenly becomes interested in finding out what she has missed all these years—and does. On this subject, more than others, anyone would be foolish to accept as gospel anything written or heard.

At this stage in widowhood, just accept as normal whatever it is you are feeling. Don't let people tell you to "use it or lose it" or throw the book of morality at you. Widows often feel guilty about going to bed with another man, but their guilt is not associated with their husbands so much as toward people right here on earth. They are uneasy with their children and family. And children in turn are just as guarded. Characteristically, mothers are not seen as sexual beings. It's embarrassing—even today. You may not be ready to explore the question of dating yet. You may not even have a sense of your physical self at this point. Before you find yourself saying "no" when you mean "yes," or "yes" when you mean "no," you may still have to resolve in your own mind questions of sin, guilt and morality. Again, there is no time frame. And sex is here to stay. The book *Sex After Sixty* is printed in large type.

Sex is here to stay.

Money, Money, Money

YOU'LL READ THAT WOMEN hold over half the wealth in this country and also that women constitute the poorest segment of the population. Poorest is more like it—women over age 65 make up the greatest part of the poverty population—with death of a spouse or divorce as the root cause. Further, because most women, regardless of age, traditionally turn to men in matters of money they are ill-equipped to manage for themselves when they become widowed.

You could be one who says, "My husband always told me about our assets and tried to get me to learn, but I just wasn't interested." Or, "We talked it over and decided that a bank trustee would be wisest for my protection and security, but I just found out that I'm making only 3 percent on my money." Or, still worse, "All I have is the insurance money, I'm too young for Social Security and too old to get a decent job; I'm frightened."

That's just a fragment of the financial disasters that befall widows. No chapter on money can include all the problems, let alone the solutions, so what I'll try to do here is offer some general advice. The first comes from the mouth of a widow who was assisted in losing $50,000 by her son-in-law: "Don't act on anyone's advice until you know what the hell you are doing." The money-foolish widow who spends her fortune on dancing lessons and the impetuous mother who divides the insurance money equally among her children, leaving herself with no capital, have become legendary.

But as a group, widows think "poor" when they are first left alone. Dancing lessons may come later. At the beginning, regardless of real income, panic sets in because, by and large, they usually are looking at a finite resource. The average widow, unlike the majority of younger women today, does not have a job that might provide an adequate ongoing income. If employed, her second-income job is likely to be low-paying. She is understandably anxious about dipping into her capital or losing it. If she is over 65, and has life savings to supplement Social Security, that is immediately dubbed her "untouchable" fund. Even when the widow has an estate that ensures her security and her accountant has explained all those zeros, she remains unsettled and acts poor long after probate and taxes are concluded. She is money inexperienced. The temptation to turn it all over to a man—son, brother, banker, or stockbroker—is overwhelmingly traditional.

When in Doubt ...

Wait! Set your nest egg to rest in some safe interest-bearing account until you become familiar with investment fundamentals and the generic vocabulary that makes it all sound so mysterious and complicated. Later, if you are still so-minded, you can turn your money over to one or more men or women because that is your decision, not because you are helpless. What you do first is believe that you can deal with money. "I am no dummy, I am no dummy." Say it until you believe it.

Don't make the mistake of taking on financial responsibilities while you are still numb and in shock. Arithmetic and numbers are too slippery then and you'll have your confidence set back to zero. But as soon as you feel able to concentrate and have located all vital documents, sit down and make an inventory of your assets and debts. This task may even take your mind off your troubles.

Don't make the mistake of taking on financial responsibilities while you are still numb and in shock.

Set aside large medical bills until you know what is covered by insurance, the figures are verified as final and you understand how bills to the estate should be paid. Astronomical hospital bills have unnecessarily shattered the composure of many widows whose sole knowledge of finances is to pay all bills by the first of the month.

If you and your husband had a business arrangement (proprietorship, partnership or corporation), especially if you operated out of your residence, you may still receive checks or cash for that business. Keep this money separate from your personal account and deposit it to the business account. Let your accountant help you with the details of what to do with money received for the business and explain how to transfer funds from the business account to your personal account as required. Working out your taxes requires a paper trail to track (trace) what has happened to the money. Just remember:

DON'T MIX BUSINESS INCOME WITH YOUR PERSONAL INCOME.

Further, if your business will be continuing now that he is gone, you'll need to work out the details of who is going to handle the financial and operational affairs to allow the business to continue successfully. Or, it could be that in consultation with your accountant and attorney you will decide to wind up the affairs of the business and close or sell it.

Figure Out Your Assets and Debts

The task of reckoning assets and debts—what one has and what one owes—is far less formidable than it seems to many widows. Get help from a family member or a friend, but don't procrastinate. You might place unopened mail in the good old shoe box for six months, write checks against no funds for six days, or zonk out on Valium forever. It's all been tried—but nothing works as well as a little knowledge and organization. If you want to be your own person, put your life back in balance, beginning with numbers. Of course you can have your daughter come over every month to balance your checkbook, but then you won't be able to say, "I'm no dummy, I'm no dummy."

Simple addition and subtraction will tell you two things you need to know: what you are worth and how your expenses balance out against your income. Aha! you say, that's the problem. Everything is tied up in probate: I don't know what I have, or alternatively, I have x number of dollars plus Social Security, but I don't know for how many years x number of dollars has to last. That kind of arithmetic is even beyond any computer, you say.

As for probate, the first thing is to do is ask questions. Don't be intimidated by lawyers and other professionals who tell you not to worry. They will free the necessary funds while the wheels of the courts slowly move on, but they don't realize that the widow would like to project to the year 2020. Insist on getting a working estimate of your funds; make them sit down with you and give you an approximation of taxes and all legal and trust charges. Seldom are these figures deliberately kept from the widow. More often it is the widow who, in her early period of disorientation, hasn't been able to absorb what was said. Later, she is embarrassed to reopen the subject lest she be thought mercenary, crass or stupid. However, better that than to spend the next year biting your fingernails, thinking poor and leaving ten-percent tips.

Now, on to assets. First of all, list all of your assets such as cash, savings, stocks and bonds, property and other personal property. For help in obtaining values, call on professionals such as your banker, auto dealer and other insiders. Many times people are surprised at their net worth and feel reassured when they realize how their equity in their house, car, and possibly stock, has appreciated over the past ten years.

Next, add up your debts (omit major medical bills). By subtracting debts from assets you will find out your net worth. Income is not an asset. Assets produce income and are what you have over and above income.

The next concern is how to spread your liquid assets out over your lifetime. This task requires more than fortune-telling cards. You could copy the financial formula of the woman who subtracted her age from 100 and divided her savings by that number to arrive at the amount she could spend each year in addition to her Social Security. "After 100," she said "who can chew steak?" Well, maybe 100 is a good enough estimate if you use that approach.

A more accepted method is first to estimate your living expenses, called a *budget*—this is something that everyone needs to do. Calculate your basic money requirement. Then determine how much money you have over and above that amount, which can become available for money growth called *investing*. The word has a flamboyant sound, but an investment may be anything from a savings account to a gold mine in Mexico. I'll get to that later.

Make a Budget

As soon as possible and so you can stop worrying, work out your budget from last year's checks—which will, of course, be different this year. But at least they will reflect your fixed living expenses. Lacking those, or if it is easier for you, get a standard budget ledger and fill in those expenses. Housing, food and medical care are the big items. Clothing, recreation, and, in general, maintaining your same living standard with as few disruptions as possible, are also important for a healthy mental attitude.

Once you estimate expenses against income you can better answer such nagging questions as "Can I afford to keep my house or my car?" and "Do I need to supplement my income with a job or family or governmental assistance?" At least half the women who immediately sell their homes, moving from their community or rushing about diminishing the quality of their lives, express regrets and can't remember a year later why they acted with such haste. Don't think poor unless it's in your budget.

Keep Records Up-to-Date

On this whole topic of money you will find nothing more important than record-keeping, whether it's for a budget, income taxes, investment purposes or keeping track of bills. The simplest bookkeeping method is the checkbook register; it may pay you in terms of convenience to keep a no-charge checking account even though the required minimum is higher. You pay everything by check and pass all income funds through that account as well, moving money in excess of the minimum to a higher-interest account when indicated. Voilà, you have on record the ins and outs, also known as *credits* and *debits* of your finances, courtesy of the bank.

The Bank

A word of caution: the banking industry has changed, and is changing drastically. Although you will need to compare services and interest rates between banks (not only do those figures change frequently, but they may also change within the same bank from day to day). Don't base your selection on interest rates alone. I found the personal assistance in the bank where my husband and I had done business for so many years a more important consideration. You may, too. For instance, it was worth a half-percent interest for me to have the bank cover my check written to the IRS—drawn from the wrong account, one with insufficient funds—with the soothing white lie that "everyone does that."

Banks do all sorts of nice things for their special customers and a special customer need not have a million dollars on deposit; she need only be friendly, courteous, and make herself known to the bank personnel. Stay away from those machines and deal with the people is my whispered recommendation.

I like the story one woman told me about shopping the banks looking for a "personal representative" similar to the person she had known before moving from another state. Finally, in one of the banks the official asked her what she was specifically looking for. She answered: "A person with a desk and a chair for me where I can sit and ask a question when I need to." As you might guess she got her personal representative on the spot.

Back to record-keeping. When your income and expenses are more complicated—and almost everyone's are these days—you need to keep a monthly ledger. There you will list the source of income and all expenses in columns according to categories: medical expenses, contributions, utilities and so on. In that way not only do you have a reference when needed, but you also have your income-tax information collected for the accountant. Many of us use red ink to post income: when you're in a hurry you can easily see just how solvent you are even without glasses.

Whatever system you use, keep it simple.

Whatever system you use, keep it simple. I can't tell you how many widows undertake systems so elaborate it would take Mr. Block himself to maintain them. Similar to the way papers disappear the more they are handled, numbers change the more they are copied. It's just one more law. Two folders, one for paid bills and one for unpaid, are really the only desk organizers you need in addition to your file. Write checks only once or twice a month, and if they don't have to be paid at once, mark the date to be mailed on the stamp corner.

Credit and Credit Cards

On the subject of credit and credit cards, you will hear that you should immediately buy something on credit to establish your rating. Nonsense. Unless you are planning to buy a big-ticket item, your local references are adequate. You'll find that credit, as always, depends on your ability to pay. Changes in the law have eliminated discriminatory attitudes. Women can now owe equally with men. As for those plastic cards, you may be able to have your joint credit cards transferred to your name with just a phone call—depending on state regulations and your credit-card company—or a visit to your bank if they were issued there. In some cases you might have to reapply, but, again, shop around and see who has the most helpful approach.

No one has to tell you that you should buy only what you can afford. Credit can be very seductive; before you tie yourself to any long-term obligation, calculate the eventual cost of credit versus cash. An impulse can turn into a second thought after you've done the arithmetic. When the cost of credit far exceeds the interest your money earns at the bank and you have the funds available, use your cash. Or, use your credit card for any advantages it may offer—but be sure to pay it on time to avoid the very high interest charges.

Money Management

Let's go on to money management: *investments, securities,* all those mysterious words. Your *capital* is money and assets beyond your month-to-month expenses. This is money you should invest, because keeping it in the sugar bowl in the back of the closet does not allow you to keep abreast of inflation. Money shrinks, and you want it to grow. For most widows capital provides interest income. That is, their funds are invested for growth or placed in interest-bearing savings accounts or certificates of deposit.

Bank accounts are government insured up to $100,000 and although interest rates fluctuate, you can depend on a return. Stocks, bonds and real estate may yield a much higher return; however, they are far riskier. Unless you either already own them or have money enough to risk, your best strategy is no strategy if your capital is under $50,000.

But even when the nest egg is bigger there are other factors to consider. For example, a younger widow with alternative income potential can take greater risks than a woman over 65 who has no replacement opportunities. A mother with underage children can take less of a chance than someone with no dependents. Then there is you and what you can live with—you'd better answer that question at your earliest opportunity.

Here are two widows: Elaine increases the mortgage on her almost-paid-for house and with the additional cash, plus her husband's insurance, invests in blue-chip stocks and bonds. She estimates that her return will offset the increased mortgage payment and yield a better return than bank or money-market interest. At risk is her house and her reserve funds, at gain is a possible higher income and increase in capital.

The other widow, Helen, pays off the mortgage and is relieved that her home is "free and clear." Her insurance money is deposited in a nice, safe bank. She gains what is most important to her, peace of mind—but loses a trip to Paris. That, very simply put, is the investment story. Here you have one think-rich widow and one think-poor widow; both are right, neither is wrong. It's a question of what you can live with—or sleep without.

Generally speaking, you can spread your money wings when you have cash assets of over six digits. If you are fortunate enough to have an estate over $100,000, you will want to explore all the investment alternatives so you can realize your best return. While you are exploring, sit on your hands. Don't even shop for an adviser, consultant or stockbroker unless you are already informed, or until you are somewhat wise and word-experienced.

Only when you know a T-bill from a Muni, when you can read stock quotations, and when you know whether you want dividend or growth stocks should you begin interviewing stockbrokers and financial advisers.

financial advisers for the right persons for you. I say this because so often people turn their affairs over to the first person who seems knowledgeable because they are overwhelmed by what appears to be an inexhaustible amount of facts and impossible decisions to be made; math anxiety one step higher. You can listen and discriminate as well as anybody else when you know what they are talking about.

Strictly speaking, a broker buys stocks and bonds and charges commission. An adviser does just that, advises, but charges a fee for services. Often the function of one blurs into the other, so you need to find out exactly what each is selling. Although investment firms offer free seminars, they are selling their own services. And when they include such freebies as dinner and champagne, the obligation to buy may handicap your judgment. If you attend such functions, leave checkbook and pen at home and sleep on your decision before acting.

Either attend enough seminars of opposing and varying kinds of investment purveyors so you may get a well-rounded education, or take a money-management course. Most community colleges offer six-week workshops that will familiarize you with the jargon and basic information. Repeat it if you are still confused; nobody is counting. There are also many excellent books available, such as The Wall Street Journal's *Guide To Understanding Money and Investing*. You should own at least one book. One thing about a book is that you can read it over and over.

Investment houses recognize that present-day widows are more sophisticated than ever before and also that they represent a good share of the investment market. To cater to this market, they employ many female brokers and salespeople. You may feel more comfortable working with a woman, but please don't make any assumptions on the basis of gender alone. In fact don't make any assumptions about *anyone* trying to sell you anything. A stockbroker is selling; anyone charging you for services—advisers, banks or financial newsletters—is selling a product. Advice, charisma or reassurance have no resale value. Examine the product.

Many people use the services of several brokers and brokerage firms so they can cross-check recommendations and research opinions. When anyone promises you double the prevailing interest,

100-percent appreciation or a return larger than is being offered elsewhere, be suspicious. Remember, the first principle of high finance is: THERE'S NO SUCH THING AS A FREE LUNCH. When you contemplate all the widows before you who lost their money through uninsured banks, second-mortgage companies with bad judgment and brokers who frittered away a bundle when given unchecked rein over an account, also be mindful of the second ancient principle: DO NOT PUT ALL YOUR EGGS INTO ONE BASKET.

Insurance Companies

We haven't mentioned insurance companies as an investment source; often they are the first to display their wares before you. Insurance companies usually offer several options to the life-insurance beneficiary and can present the widow with her first dilemma. You will be asked whether you wish to receive the benefits in cash, as an annuity or purchase life insurance for yourself or for your children. You may be presented with still other options. One insurance plan that is too often overlooked is to have the company retain the money at interest until you decide. That's a good idea for a young widow who is debating between an annuity or cash. All options should be closely examined and compared with other market investments. You may need help from a knowledgeable person before deciding. Many widows end up with insurance policies they don't need and decisions they don't need to be making so early.

When you are ready to take fiscal responsibility for yourself you may find the prospect more frightening than the reality. As a widow you may find your income diminished and be required to reassess your lifestyle. You'll find there are many possibilities, none of which demand that you think poor. Alternatively, you may find that your income has not lessened, but perhaps increased. You could be staring at even more possibilities and decisions. In either case your only real handicap is *ignorance.*

Try not to be hampered by what you think your husband would have done or would want you to do. It's a fast-changing world and you are the one living in it. There may be moments when you'd love to see civilization go back to those simple, little, blue trading beads. But once you get started, you'll find managing your money is just one more of the opportunities for challenge.

'Tis the Season to be Jolly?

HOLIDAYS TEST THE SPIRIT. They are double-bind days: You want to be part of the festivities and at the same time pull the blankets up over your head until it all goes away. For the newly widowed, the days from Thanksgiving until New Year's could easily be turned in for scrap.

"Share with a person who is alone this year" is the sentiment that gets sprinkled around like Christmas glitter. We hear it from the media, the pulpit and the Rotary Club newsletter prior to all the traditional family holidays—Thanksgiving, Christmas, Hanukkah. The words are guaranteed to turn any new widow back to mush. All the seasonal goodwill and the well-intentioned people looking for needy recipients on whom they can lavish that goodwill are small comfort to her. She would much rather be sitting next to her husband on this holiday looking around for *their* lonely person.

Being taken in by the cheerful congregation is definitely patronizing.

Nothing works and everything hurts. Participating in the holiday dinner of former friends is a lonely affair. Being taken in by the cheerful congregation is definitely patronizing.

My House or Yours?

Having all the family come home for the holidays also has its drawbacks. The bosom of the family falls short of expectations. The kids, worried about Mom's first Christmas without Dad, all congregate as they once did so Mom will not be lonesome. Lonesome is one thing Mom is not. She is too busy cleaning the house, renting foldaway cots, shopping for supplies and gifts, and practicing not crying. The grandchildren, beautiful and blessed, run through the house continuously and circularly. They have been carefully rehearsed not to ask for Grandpa. At some point, either all together as planned, or individually, the kids variously advise Mom to sell the house, not sell the house, take a trip, move to Florida, or "Come live with us, the children need you; Brenda is going back to work." Finally, they all leave, and Mom cries to see them go, but she is not so much lonely as—what's the word?—*exhausted!*

In the early years of widowhood there is a need to recapture past traditions and carry on.

Or, Mom is invited to one of the children's for the holiday. Here she also practices not crying and not interfering. Everyone is solicitous and loving. Why does she feel part of her is away and missing? "I know I should be grateful to have such a wonderful family," she says to herself. The truth is that the trip was horrendous, the plane hours late, and now two weeks later she is not wearing Billy's cold quite as well as he did. Everyone tried but no one really had a good time.

Your first holiday scenario may be quite different, but with minor changes for sex, plot and date most of us are living it or have lived it. In the early years of widowhood there is a need to recapture past traditions and carry on. We used to think that Christmas was suicide time for lonely people, but statistics don't bear out that premise. In truth, most of us muddle through much better than we think we will.

You May Only Want Quiet

Jolliness may not be for you this year. Nor is there something wrong with you if you do not feel enthusiastic or grateful about sharing other people's traditions (even your children's). The fact is we really don't want to be part of someone else's tradition. If we can't have our own, we'd just as soon play it down. Shed a tear or two and indulge in a little self-pity, knowing that for the most part it's a time for sweet remembrances and softly closing old doors behind us as we open those ahead.

Do as you like. Say "no" if you wish. Say "yes" if you want. Give your own party if you choose, or get jolly good and mad because you cannot have what you most want. As impossible as it seems, in time you will find your way to a different place at the feast.

Give your own party if you choose, or get jolly good and mad because you cannot have what you most want.

Letter to Martin

A Journal Entry

Dear Martin,

Uncoupling. I used that word today talking to a woman who is having a terrible time accepting her divorce, and the word has stayed in my head all day the way a tune will do sometimes. I think that's what's happening to us.

It started not too long ago when the new baby was born. His name is Peter Martin, and at first sight I searched his every inch for you. Ah yes, your hands, your big toe, could that be your chin? But he's just a little baby, and who knows? If he is to inherit something of you, I hope it will be—like you—to be his own person.

I was there in California the night he was born. Paul returned late from the hospital filled to overflowing from having been part of this miracle; he couldn't stop talking about how wonderful Marcia had been and how remarkable was this child who calmly looked about the room sizing up his new world with great aplomb—already an observer.

It was late but I couldn't get to sleep—Paul's excitement stayed in the air—and as I lay in bed I waited to be overtaken with the sadness I've come to know as your absence. Instead, I felt warm and glad to be alive and looking forward to holding our new baby. And I knew suddenly what was wrong: I felt sad for *you and what you were missing.* I was happy—unilaterally, as they say—for myself.

I think I'm saying good-bye to you in a way I never knew would happen. A week ago, when I received notice of an appointment to a state commission, I once again had the sensation of leaving you behind. On first impulse I wanted to rush over to your office: "Get your hat, let's celebrate." I didn't celebrate either, but I felt bad for you; you loved any excuse for a good dinner and a bottle of wine.

Tonight on the local news when one of your least-favorite city-hall political figures put his foot in his mouth, I laughed out loud and said out loud—to the dog I suppose—"Martin would have loved that."

And now for no reason I know—but of course, it's the divorcee whose husband dumped her for his dental assistant—I've been thinking. What if I had been the one to die, what would you be doing? Out to dinner with a tall brunette, I betcha. Oh, not too young, you liked your women mature, intelligent and subtly sexy; the phone would be ringing off the hook. All those women who looked so crestfallen when I'd move up to you at those big cocktail parties and knew you meant it when you said, "This is my wife," would be calling.

What else? Would you have gone off on a sailboat as you always wanted, to law school, or—another well-worn fantasy—written poetry? (How is it that you wrote your best sonnets in the bathroom?) It's hard to know; with me dead and you alive, you would be a different person. And that, my love, is the tune I've been hearing in my head all day. I am becoming a different person—uncoupling.

A line from *Cyrano de Bergerac* comes to my mind. God, how you loved that play. You must have read it to me a hundred times—all the parts; I'd have to fight you to play that dumb Rocanne. Was the great frustration of your life that you never played Cyrano? I have a picture of you, wigged and mustached, playing the Count de Guiche, when our ATC did the play—just before you died. You got killed in the first act. I wouldn't want to hurt your feelings, but you got the part because you were old enough to have been a fencer when colleges had fencing teams and because you were crazy enough to be the first president of ATC when it had no money, no stage, no audience, just actors.

Anyway, remember the line in the long speech Cyrano gives summing up his philosophy of life: He will toady to no man nor compromise that which is of value to him—Sandy read it at your memorial service—Cyrano says, and I hear your voice: "Some make a single sonnet serve a lifetime. That's not for me." No, that was never for you. Nor, my dear, is it for me.

Love,

Me

Part 3

From Widowhood to Selfhood

THE PAGES THAT FOLLOW ARE INTENDED to give you a wider perspective on growing single. For widowhood is more than coping and overcoming. It is a bona fide life stage where the choice is not limited to replacing one partner with another. Or, failing that, remaining a wife without a husband forever after. Rather, this is a stage with unlimited potential, many choices and—shocking as it may sound—a stage when woman may live happily with or without a man.

You were dragged unwillingly into this so-called *life passage,* but once here it can become an opportunity to discover the person buried under so many layers of daughter, wife, mother. It can be a time to explore your own inner boundaries and experience the thrill of approaching new experiences, albeit very carefully and with your heart in your throat. Possibly one day you'll meet yourself coming around the block and hardly recognize yourself and ask, "Is that me?" You'll never be the same, not after you've made the distance from widowhood to singlehood.

As always there will be good days and bad days, fears and tears, and all the little inequities that comprise life at any time. But it can be your time to discover you are not a mechanical idiot or a financial simpleton. There are worse things than sleeping in the middle of your bed and not knowing whether you snore. That saying adieu to sex does not make your cheeks fall in and your hair fall out. That it's the best time for making new friends: brief hour-long friends in foreign places, dinner friends, go-to-the-theater friends, I-need-to-talk friends and others you would not have tolerated when you had your one best friend.

Most unexpectedly rewarding, though, is becoming acquainted with solitude and having the time for it. Widowhood is not a way station where life is put on hold waiting for the return of the status quo. It has status now; it is a stage of choices. As a single woman your life will be different; it can be exciting, rewarding and happy. As was always true, you have many directions in which to go and many ways to become uniquely you. The difference now is that it is up to you alone. That's a new brand of "alone," isn't it?

As a single woman your life will be different; it can be exciting, rewarding and happy.

Uncoupling

THE BIBLE *records no single animal* having been permitted entry onto Noah's Ark; they came in twos. There is, and always has been, a certain deficiency attached to singleness. Look in the thesaurus and you come up with words like *spinster, bachelor, unmarried, wifeless, old maid:* all derogatory and hinting of defectiveness. Additionally, we have been conned by movies, T.V., popular music, vacation ads and other profit-making motives into believing that happiness marches two by two and anything less is loneliness. Bridal schools do not offer post-graduate courses; they end happily ever after.

So it is not entirely a condition of self-pity or paranoia that causes the widow to feel a misfit. It is fact that half of a couple does not equal one, it equals 50 percent of one. Because we live in a coupled world, no one who has lived the coupled life with any degree of satisfaction can properly project the stark reality of noncoupled life.

One can fantasize what life would be like going it alone, as most of us did at one time or another, and sincerely sympathize with the new widow, as most of us also did in the past. But we are unprepared for the small, sharp shocks: walking into an empty house and realizing, with sudden and full impact, that it may always feel empty. We are unprepared for the silence of our voice and the crackled "Hello" that greets the first telephone caller of the day. Even more devastating are the social differences that become more and more apparent as we venture back onto the scene.

Making a brave reentry into society as a single at those big, impersonal cocktail parties, church socials, holiday celebrations or, in fact, any large gathering where people come and go in couples, is an assured depressant. Here, we are attached, but to a glass of whatever it is we are drinking, holding on for dear life. Here, we are acting just like a real person, but singularly aware of the tautness of the trying-so-hard mask on our face. Acquaintances stop to tell us how wonderful we look, and because an acceptable grieving period (three months) has passed, no one mentions *his* name. At no time can you turn to that best friend and say, "Let's get out of here," and giggle about Suzi's upside-down false eyelashes or Joe's skewed hairpiece. You come and go alone, and I mean *alone,* no matter how many people are about.

Old Patterns Don't Fit

Initially, we try bravely facing the world, including bravely trying to lead the life we led. It doesn't work. After a while, the widow of experience learns to pick and choose. She learns to avoid situations that induce the blues unless there is some compensating benefit—fantastic food or interesting people—to make it worthwhile. She also learns—and no one ever told her about this—how to enter a room on her own and depart alone. Even more difficult, she learns to ask for assistance without upsetting her delicate independent-dependent balance. We're haunted by the image of the pesky little widow tagging along, but with experience, even strong survivors recognize their own individual limitations.

> *Initially, we try bravely facing the world, including bravely trying to lead the life we led. It doesn't work.*

I think back on one awful night and recall the big fund-raising dinner for the civic theater, an annual event we, as a couple, had always attended because my husband had been one of the founders of the group. "Keep going," I told myself. "Fake it until you make it," as another widow advised. So, I had gone—all gussied up and by myself. Unfortunately, no one had thought to tell me that the evening was to include a tribute to my husband—for which I was as unprepared as my Siamese cat when she gave birth to a litter of seven. A moving event, but what does one do next? I was practiced enough to hold head up and eyes down for the remaining program, but not for managing the flood of self-pity overflowing my banks. I was alone in a crowd of friends (friends?), with the carcass of a tear-dampened Rock Cornish hen my only companion. I wondered how

I could get out of there without invoking pity for the poor woman—the only odd woman on earth—driving off into the night all by herself. I hated them all, every coupled one of them.

Now I have better sense and would either arrange beforehand to go with some other couples or invite one of my acquired single acquaintances to go along. Two make a couple, you know. In fact, one woman I know whose invitation to a black-tie wedding-anniversary party at a fancy country club read ". . . and Guest" brought a woman friend and rather enjoyed the mixed reaction.

The coupled dinner party of old is another downer. For a while we and our friends maintained the old routine. They make a valiant effort to include the widow and the widow pulls herself together to reciprocate. With some small exceptions, however, the evening suffers from an excess of pleasantness, too much smiling, too much helpfulness and forced caring. After a time, almost by mutual consent, and after everyone has assured the widow that she will always be a part of the old gang, the old club, the old discussion group, the old square-dance class, the old inseparable sixsome—the old groupings fade out, and new ones grow in their places.

The widow may be dumped by the old crowd because she is a sexual threat or a grim reminder of awaiting reality, as legend has it. Most widows say the old coupled friends become a little—well—boring. Making what is known as *women-talk,* no longer relevant to her present lifestyle, while the men, on their side of the room, make male-talk, just isn't gratifying enough to be worth the trouble.

New Ways of Socializing

With time, it becomes easier to maintain the relationships you value and in the manner you value them. Although it may take some doing, once you make it clear to good coupled friends that you wish to pay your own share, it can become acceptable and enjoyable for you to go out socially together. There are some women, however, who say neither they nor their friends like such arrangements. These women prefer to reciprocate either with an at-home dinner or advance arrangements at a restaurant. I think that eliminates spontaneous and informal get-togethers, but that's up to each individual.

One workable method for entertaining couples at home is with an annual open house, cocktail party, buffet, barbecue or anything that's informal. People more or less entertain each other, help themselves and leave you free to buzz around taking care of details without feeling like a wagon with a missing wheel. That's my system for keeping up with old friends as well as new ones. Then, when it's all over, I feel socially successful and too tired to miss the man who used to play host to my hostess.

> *Curiously, my yearly New Year's Day party has become such an anticipated event that my guests often R.S.V.P. before I've sent out the invitations.*

Curiously, my yearly New Year's Day party has become such an anticipated event that my guests often R.S.V.P. before I've sent out the invitations. "We meet such interesting people at your party," everyone tells me. And they're right, because mixed with all the interesting couples are the interesting and fascinating single women—many widowed—whom I've come to know only since becoming one of them.

Obviously, one's social life is different as a single; the ways in which we entertain and are entertained change drastically. Without question you will forgo, miss and yearn for many of the things you used to do. Some women say they miss dancing the most; they never dance anymore. Or they miss a night out on the town: after-theater restaurants, fancy affairs, typical boy/girl functions. That's when they sing, "They're singing songs of love, but not for me." And some of your social life *isn't* different. The whole trick lies in discriminating between what makes you miserable and what pleases you. Why, unless you absolutely must, go to the Heart Fund Ball and sit there like a lump waiting for a charitable partner to waltz you around once? Why go to the football game, which you never cared for anyway, because you and your husband and the other four couples had established the tradition of attending together ever since high school? Let it go.

New Activities

On the other hand, there is no reason to wrap yourself up in a cocoon. There's even less excuse for settling into total passivity, where one goes no place unless carted to and fro by family or friends. Such widows give all of us a bad name and tend to overshadow all the gutsy ladies, such as the woman, who at age 80, learned to ride a bus and manage her own affairs and recreation. Both the deposed wife-queen and the rest of us poor serfs discover— sooner or later—that happiness does not lie in listening to old love songs.

There are many activities you can do by yourself and many more for which you can find suitable companions. I like to go to the movies alone and eat my popcorn in peace. I park my car close to a light and lock it. Some women take courses and attend lectures on their own, replace dancing with Jazzercise classes, and continue with whatever former socializing is feasible and comfortable. Most urgent, however, is building your own network of single friends and couples with whom you can go out.

Most urgent, however, is building your own network of single friends and couples with whom you can go out.

You can meet other single women in classes and clubs or at work who are also looking for new friendships and partners for theater subscriptions, bingo, concerts or horse racing, to mention a few gala events that you needn't give up. Widows' support groups may provide a bountiful supply of new companions and new undertakings. One group met regularly to play cards and go to "nice" restaurants where the women normally hesitated to go unaccompanied and where many admitted their husbands would not have taken them.

So it's not all sour grapes. Many women state that, as a group, women are the more interesting of the two sexes. Among older single women you'll often hear one say, "I'd much rather spend an evening with one or two women; the men you meet can be so dull." And most of them mean it. Those who have adjusted to singlehood credit their success to not only having made a break from the old social patterns, but having made close ties with other women. "And if I get to feeling sorry for myself when I'm out with couples," one widow said, "I just take a good look at each man in the room and say, Thank God I don't have to go home with him tonight."

A Life of One's Own

THE WIDOW TALKS ABOUT HER LOST IDENTITY a lot. "Who am I?" she asks. She feels out of balance—off-center—socially and internally. No longer defined as a wife, her sense of self is disrupted: "I used to write 'housewife' on applications where it called for occupation, but I'm not a wife now. I don't even know how to fill in that space," one widow laments.

"Homemaker," someone answers. "That's what you were and still are."

"No," says the first widow, "I'm not making a home for anyone. Ask any man who he is, and he'll say, 'engineer,' 'businessman,' or 'retired.' But us, we're nobody."

That may be a gloomy assessment, but nonetheless many women do feel bereft of their identity when they become widows. Possibly young widows of today, because they are more vocationally achieving and socially independent—many have experienced the dissolution of a previous marriage—will feel less hollow under the same circumstances. It's interesting to observe the young superwomen—lawyers, doctors, mothers, wives—and see who feels responsible for picking up the lemons on the way home.

Nevertheless, social changes have come about. Certainly the widow of 100 years ago had a tougher time of it. The pioneer widow took in boarders, ran a whorehouse, took in laundry, took over the ranch, taught school or remarried. Survival took priority over identity. The Eastern widow more often cried into her black-bordered handkerchief and went to live with relatives. Poor soul. (Thank heavens no one has thought of black Kleenex tissues.)

So why—in spite of the feminist gains within the past three decades—do women feel so imperfect as to envision themselves primarily as wives without husbands when they are widowed? (I know it came as a surprise to me that I could so abruptly feel less important, more helpless as a widow than as a wife, but I did.) Psychologists postulate that relationships are more important to women, that they are the natural "givers," and that women measure their importance by how successfully they attract men. Therefore, without a man, a widow becomes a lesser creature.

Whether female traits are inherited or learned—and the debate is everlasting—women define themselves by their roles. A man's sense of identity is not essentially dependent on his role as "husband," nor so closely enmeshed in his relationship with a woman. Women, however, have their roles more clearly defined by behavior and their emotional relationships. In the more or less natural progression of life, as they advance from daughter to wife to mother, their positioning provides form and meaning to their lives. While one woman's individual concept and expectations for her role varies from another, her ego and sense of herself is framed by her current role. She is a *mother,* a *wife,* she knows who she is. But as a widow she is disconnected from any point of reference. She is a *widow!* And who is that? A widow is someone else. It's not a job, it has no status, and I don't want it. You can have it.

Shaping a Separate Identity

Thus widowhood begins with a minus of "me" and can only end with a plus when the widow gives up being her husband's wife and shapes a separate identity for herself. Some pooh-pooh the notion that a woman gains status and identity through her husband. That's the Dark Ages, one of my friends argued. Yet she was the very one who, when her husband died, interrupted work on her doctorate to complete his unfinished play. Nor is she the only woman who ever gave up her work to carry on her husband's career and bury herself, not him. You see it in politics and on the farm, and where women make speeches and sing songs. In some sacrificial manner they devote themselves to perpetuating his image as though they are the shadow and he the substance.

But most women with the passage of time have a boundless capacity for reconstituting themselves. Ultimately the loyalty-driven woman realizes she can, if she wishes, run for election in her own right, speak her own words and earn her own medals. On a less lofty plane, most of us come to the same conclusion and begin to shape a new life that, be it ever so humble, is our own. Two years! Many women say that it took them two years to slough off the widow image and to realize *widow* is only a word, not a condition. Queen Victoria took more time and the 60-year-old woman who learned to drive took less.

> *Most women with the passage of time have a boundless capacity for reconstituting themselves.*

Granted, some women never achieve that new sense of self and are forever widows; they are helpless, spiritless, and the despair of those who care about them. They seem to derive some benefit from having bent to the winds of misfortune. We want to shake them and say, "Hey, you are somebody," but they are not ready. When you ask women who have put aside their symbolic widow's weeds how they view themselves now, their answers reflect pride and a revived sense of worth. It's heartening to hear them.

"I'm a woman who has lived through the worst that can happen, and I'm here to tell the story."

"I'm different than I used to be. I lost a lot, but I gained an appreciation of my own ability."

"Who am I? I'm a person, me. I think for myself and act for myself. In my whole life I never did that before."

"I'm Judith, the Same. My life has changed, but I'm proud of what I've done on my own and feel good about myself."

"I'm a single woman. I might remarry someday, but I won't settle for less than I deserve."

Few of us are so self-reliant that we happily put aside the yearning for an intimate relationship. But what makes women extraordinary is their continuing gift for making other tributary relationships. That quality enables them to make this phase of their lives—let's call it *after widowhood*—full-flowing. They accomplish this by giving to others, forever connecting with people. While they may retain a bigger core of private self, that core is less needy.

Helping Others

In support groups, widows clearly and visibly help themselves by helping others, as others might do through volunteer work and other outreach efforts. As widows reshape their lives they carve out the makings of a new identity. They become the grandmother who takes the kids camping, the docent who brings snakes to the fourth-grade children, and the Mobile-Meal lady who always has time to listen. There was one woman in her 70s, always in demand as a part-time bookkeeper for the small-business person needing rescuing, who in her past life had kept the books for "my husband's business." Another healed dispirited seniors with her inspirational yoga classes. Not the close coupling of the past, but then what's a relationship? To feel needed and loved and warmed. Should you ask these women who they are, they won't say, "just a widow . . . a nobody."

The dry statistics of the U.S. Census Bureau tell us that almost half of all married women over 65 will become widows and will outlive their husbands by 18 years. That's an awful lot of widows and a sizable chunk of life. We jolly well better not say "nobody."

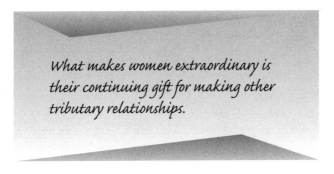

What makes women extraordinary is their continuing gift for making other tributary relationships.

To Work, Volunteer or Play?

EMPLOYMENT IS AN ECONOMIC NECESSITY for many widows; it's hardly a choice. For others a job means prestige, status or "something to do to keep from going crazy." Whatever your motivation, whether you need to supplement Social Security, fully support yourself and your young children or preserve your self-esteem, your first priority may be employment. And if you have never worked or are re-entering the labor market after an absence, the prospect is as intimidating as the first day of kindergarten.

You may already be employed (over half the women with school-age children are working) and your job may dovetail with your needs as far as salary and schedule are concerned. If so, you're lucky. The usual story women tell is that theirs was the second income and not a career job. Now they are locked into dead-end tedium and are apprehensive about seeking alternative employment.

When employment is concerned, so many widows, young and old, talk much more than they do. Doing is that threatening. And talking is good for a while, because until she is able to concentrate, regain her sense of humor and feel connected to the mainstream, no widow is what they call *work ready*. But know the difference between procrastination and being unready; you sometimes have to give yourself a push by taking a preliminary step. Set a date, have your hair done, schedule a related appointment, and do it.

If you've had work on your mind, you'll probably notice that there is a whole industry looking for your business: career counseling, vocational testing, employment workshops, new methodology, and stacks of magazines and books. Some you might find very worthwhile and some not. Anyone promising to turn you into top-executive material through some kind of magic is guaranteeing his employment, not yours. Likewise, an expensive battery of tests may not be worth the outlay because, typically, those interest tests return your own input. You already know whether you like to work with people or things and whether you'd rather be a brain surgeon or a pilot. Aptitude tests provide mainly general, not specific, information. However, if you think a battery of tests will be helpful, testing is usually available through college counseling departments at a lower cost and through state employment offices and special governmental programs. So before you invest in a costly process, investigate other sources as well. That's also true of employment agencies; their fee may outlast the job, so carefully read what you are contracting for. And don't overlook the many excellent books available at libraries and bookstores.

What Do You Want from a Job?

Because job hunting eventually boils down to your own input and your own effort, regardless of how you approach it, you'll want a clear view of your particular values. Income, job security, social and physical environment, personal fulfillment and time schedules are all separate considerations. Sometimes you can't have it all. You may not be able to satisfy more than one condition at a time, although you certainly can expect to shift directions in your lifetime and plan ahead for changes.

One working mother was satisfied because she was advancing educationally and vocationally while working at a dull job that permitted her to be home after school. Another, with no future plans, felt cheated and bitter. The women, coincidentally, were co-workers. That's why it helps to have a sense of purpose in mind; a compromise is more palatable when it is a matter of choice.

Paradoxically, the employment section of the newspaper is not the best place to look for employment unless you have well-defined work skills, experience and references. It's competitive—80 people might apply for the same job. That can be time-consuming and discouraging.

Your chances improve if you know the kind of position you're seeking and approach your market more directly; the best way is through a personal reference. That's why looking for a job is an inadequate vocational choice; you need to ask friends and casual acquaintances for names and contacts in specific areas. "I'm looking for a receptionist's job. Do you know anyone I could talk to?" "By the way, I'm thinking of changing law firms. Have any ideas?"

Older women who see themselves as vocationally déclassé are foolishly embarrassed to ask one of their husband's friends for leads, but that can be your best bet. Ask them for the names of people you can approach for the kind of job you have in mind, and you'll usually find instant allies. Next, search out the market and apply directly to firms and companies either in person or through letters to a specific person who is in charge.

If you have no skill or training and wonder what you could possibly do, you can adopt the system of observing other people's jobs and talking to them about their duties and qualifications—like a research project. Returning home from a family visit, one middle-aged widow stopped to watch an airport information attendant at work and thought, "There's something I could do." She talked to the attendant, who was enthusiastic about her position and the company management policies and who also mentioned that there was an opening for a relief person. So luggage in hand, the widow walked over to the personnel office. She started working the next day.

Many women have talents and abilities they can convert into a small business that requires little capital and that may be operated from the home.

Don't worry about resumes unless you are a professional where such presentations are routinely expected. The widow who is looking for a job for the first time looks foolish with a resume that equates her former homemaking tasks with what is supposed to be job-related. Some workshops use that approach, and while your morale will be boosted when you realize that if you managed a household budget you understand arithmetic, an employer will not be impressed. Talk it up during an interview, but unless you have experience and references that are current and relevant, a neatly typed page giving your vital statistics and educational and vocational background is all the resume you'll need.

Dress conservatively, wear little jewelry and use makeup sparingly. Women who have been away from the work force try to compensate by dressing in the latest fashion, splashing on the newest scent and streaking their faces with what's new in eye makeup. It is certainly unflattering as well as inappropriate for an interview.

When you've had an interview and are interested in the job, write a note to the interviewer thanking him or her and indicate your interest in the job or for working with that particular company.

Many women have talents and abilities they can convert into a small business that requires little capital and that may be operated from the home—typing, catering, art classes and tutoring, to name a few. For instance, there are three successful homemade-salsa ventures in my neighborhood. For those with investment capital, there are many good entrepreneurial opportunities. Thirty percent of owner-operated businesses are run by women. There are federal programs for small-business and business-women's networks that have helpful mentor programs and support systems if you're thinking along those lines. Contact your local Chamber of Commerce for names of the latter.

Volunteering

Another excellent way to break into the labor market is through a volunteer job. Every volunteer is also a potential employee; she's on the spot with experience should a job open up. Not every volunteer, however, cares to become employed, and if you are fortunate enough to be able to work for the sake of feeling productive and contributing you are well occupied.

> *Every volunteer is also a potential employee.*

Let's talk about volunteer jobs. Most people think of hospital pink (blue or gray) ladies when the word *volunteer* is mentioned, and it may be that's what you think of too. Frankly, that is not my favorite volunteer job for widows who have spent months and years caring for a sick husband or for those who want to become more involved in the total operation of an agency or organization.

If you care to learn something new and challenging there are many areas where volunteers are performing essential and interesting work. These include being a victim advocate or child advocate for the courts or social agencies, a teaching aide, library aide or museum docent. There you also come away with an education in art or natural history. You can also help out at parks and recreation facilities, teach senior courses and so on.

One 70-year-old is having the time of her life working at the zoo. Almost every community has a volunteer bureau that will match your interest with community needs—on a trial basis (so you won't end up a dropout). If your community doesn't have such an agency, there is a volunteer job waiting for you: Start one.

Overall, the job you take should return something in kind: growth, gratification and the opportunity to be with people. That's your salary. As a steady diet, just being a nice guy becomes dull. If you feel obliged to help out at some very routine job, place a time limit on your contract so you won't feel like such a villain when you leave. Otherwise, you'll find yourself sitting alone in a cubbyhole at the church office answering the phone every Monday for the rest of your life like one woman who couldn't say "I quit."

Be selective in choosing a volunteer job, but also be dependable; you have to be professional to receive full pay.

Play

In play, we're talking about recreation, education, travel and having time for yourself and those you enjoy. Curiously, many widows see playing as the opposite of grieving and force themselves into busy play. "It's time I started doing something for myself," they say. Leisure activities should indeed do something *for* you, but not *to* you. A constant round of luncheons, shopping excursions, movies and passive TV does more for your waistline than your soul, but it's a phase many widows go through and—please—come out of. It's almost as depressing as sitting around all day waiting for the world to end.

We require balance in our lives between working and playing, giving and taking, and being busy and being quiet.

There is no one too old, too rich, too poor or too stupid to participate in meaningful life experiences. A 90-year-old woman called me one day to tell me about an emergency alert service for people living alone that she thought would be helpful to new widows. Her name sounded familiar, and I remembered that she used to raise funds for supplying oxygen to needy home patients, and asked her if she was still active in that cause. No, she told me, she was blind now and homebound so she used the telephone to help people and keep in touch with what was going on.

If you are reasonably mobile, there is so much to do these days. All sorts of activities are free and available. You'll find them listed in your local newspaper, library, community centers, YWCAs and city recreation departments. Colleges and junior colleges cater to adult students and are offering more and more noncredit courses for them in every subject, from baroque music to cake decorating.

And there is an ever-increasing number of older women working towards college degrees just for the pleasure of learning. Join a chorus if you like to sing, a musical group if you play an instrument, participate in a Great Decisions group if you are interested in foreign affairs. Plus there is an endless variety of hobby groups, including plate collecting. Welcome Wagon, the organization for newcomers to a neighborhood, or the Chamber of Commerce have listings of what's happening. If you're homebound, organize a needlework group or, as one woman did, a book-discussion club. And forever and always advance in the pleasure of solitude: reading, thinking, walking, daydreaming.

If you think of your day—your life—as being full of empty holes, time is an enemy. (What is it that Shakespeare has Richard saying? "Once I wasted time, now time wastes me.") But if you view time now as newly minted, there are so many ways to spend it. You can work for money or for love, you may meditate, communicate, advocate, educate, participate—none are mutually exclusive, you know—but don't just sit there twiddling your thumbs.

> *If you think of your day—your life—as being full of empty holes, time is an enemy.*

Rebuilding a Nest

"DON'T DO A *THING* FOR A YEAR." Unless you have been living on the moon, you have been warned repeatedly about not making changes during the first year of widowhood. Well, it's true, the newly widowed are inclined, to put it kindly, to be a bit obsessive, a little single-minded in purpose.

I can tell you about the woman who unloaded her entire portfolio of stocks and bonds without regard for market conditions because "I wanted all my money in the bank so I would know what I had." It was also shortsighted for another to sell the business she and her husband had been successfully operating (and which she could have continued) within seven weeks of his death. "Life is over," she incorrectly predicted.

Many of us, midway between confusion and craziness, charge into action with the intensity of a steamroller. Our bills are lined up, paid and twice paid with the next mail, plants are overwatered on a regular schedule, and the contents of storage sheds that have lain fallow for years disposed of. My husband had a pistol collection; the guns were unassembled in a locked box in a locked storage closet where they had been sitting since the end of World War II. "Sell guns" was on an early TO DO list ahead of "Buy milk." I still don't understand the delusional logic of that priority, but I did it. Perhaps it had to do with putting my little nest in survival order.

In that first year there is no decision more important, or more difficult, than where to live.

Because habitat is one of the big-change areas, it is where so many widows go wrong. In that first year there is no decision more important, or more difficult, than where to live. Home Sweet Home without a man around the house is the first lesson in living alone. Even when there are children or other adults still living at home, the widow classifies herself as "alone." The reason for caution about making 148 changes is that her whole perception about being alone changes so that today's solutions may very well turn out to be tomorrow's mistakes. So, before you sell, buy, move or give property away (commonly regretted), pause and count to 10,000. Leave a wide margin on any plan for conflict, indecision and your everlasting potential for growth.

Women who had never in their lives spent a night alone are surprised when after a while they cease being fearful and anxious. They are also surprised at how their way of life shifts and how their requirements change. Joining the Audubon Society converted one confirmed city apartment dweller into the owner of a little house in the country where she pursued her newly acquired interest in bird identification.

Unless it is essential then, allow time for your psyche to simmer down. In the meantime, answer some questions for yourself. You are more rational than you were in the beginning and can rely on your judgment now. Can you afford to stay where you are? That's the first question. If, for instance, there is a burdensome mortgage or killer apartment payment that is a financial drain, then sell or rent the house or move out of the apartment as soon as possible. No sense in sitting there with a big house, swimming pool, pool table and full bar—or the equivalent—for 365 days, depleting the insurance money while waiting for year's end. Sounds sad, but it actually happens.

Likewise, there is no sense remaining in a location when you have no strong ties of friendship and family or a desire to remain. Often, such is the case when people have relocated because of a job retirement. "I never wanted to live so far away from the girls, but he insisted, and I guess I should stay out of respect to him." Another sad story . . . whereas the woman from Buffalo, New York, who moved herself and her arthritis to Florida in spite of admonishments about the before-a-year rule suffered no remorse.

Stay or Go?

If you were to relocate, where would you go? What would you do there? Close your eyes and picture what a day would be like in that environment. What is the transportation system like? Will you be mobile? How about noise and air pollution? Climate? Friends?

Some situations can be tried and tested. One summer I rented an apartment for a month in San Francisco, close to my son and his family, as an experiment in relocating. I learned that what I missed most was not my familiar surroundings, but my sense of identity. Fractured though it was, my sense of myself was reduced in that new setting and "Grandma" just didn't fill all the spaces—even in San Francisco.

You can save yourself grief and remorse with a trial period both before you buy and before you sell. For example, had the many sorry widows rented their homes in Kansas City or tested the waters in Dallas before committing themselves to moving closer to their families, they would not be feeling so misplaced. The same caution may be used when you're planning to purchase a home in a new location: First, rent.

When you are considering a change of dwelling, don't overlook the financial consequences as well as the total environment. Seek expert information on renting and buying. Learn the differences between houses, condominiums, town houses and mobile homes—particularly when you're considering a senior community or retirement home where the lifestyle is different from what you've known.

Mobile-home parks are popular with many widows because they require a minimal investment, and the close proximity of one mobile home to another offers security and little maintenance. The amenities of the various parks, however, differ. So do the costs and fees. Some have well-executed recreation programs, but others have

Because there is no way to predict what will satisfy you, listen to your own inner voice and trust your instinctive feelings.

those facilities on paper, not on the grounds. Examine the fee schedule closely and understand the difference between "available" and "accessible." Get the facts, visit, and talk to enough people living there to obtain a fair sampling. Because there is no way to predict what will satisfy you, listen to your own inner voice and trust your instinctive feelings. I have seen many happily transferred widows who are grateful for having new surroundings. I also have heard many lament, "I never should have left." Moving never eliminates *all* the negatives, so if you are weighing one consideration against another, don't overlook the obvious one of having to change the bathwater rather than the baby. In the long run, you may very well be better off staying where you are and tailoring your home to your present requirements.

There aren't any statistics on how many widows remain in their homes after their husbands die, but I'll bet most do. It's easier, less expensive, requires no decisive action and presents fewer imponderables. If there is one single piece of wisdom to pass on to those who choose to do so, it is: Concentrate on developing new and crucial relationships with such people as plumbers, electricians, carpenters and one really significant handyman. If you own a car, find an honest, compassionate auto mechanic. Invest in an alarm system, automatic garage door, sturdy locks and other safety devices that will make you feel safe. An alarm system may be expensive, but it is worth it, as I discovered after one burglary and one robbery. (Know the difference? A robbery is when you're in the house.) See pages 62-63 and 220-222 for more information about home security.

As you will notice, the running theme here is:

HOME IS WHERE YOU ARE,
MAKE IT WORK FOR YOU, MAKE IT YOURS.

Certainly don't wait all year to establish your own home. In fact, the sooner the better. Unfortunately, many widows feel bound and obligated to preserve visibly the memory of their husbands with walls of pictures, awards, plaques and yards of memorabilia. Their homes become shrines and they, surrounded by pictures and relics of the past, are the keepers of the past. If that makes you feel glad, not sad; fulfilled, not empty, that's okay. But you should consider that there are other ways to cherish the past and better ways to live the future.

Suit Yourself

I am also 100 percent in favor of the nonpreservation of rooms and space that no longer serve their former purpose. The study, the unused workshop with its unused tools, and the old pickup truck all have conversion possibilities that you might think about. Don't forget, you can always sell unused items. One woman who turned her husband's office into a potting shed-plant room started a cactus collection that has since grown to become an absorbing business. You might think that it is easier to close the door on an unused room and put it out of your mind; not true! The door that needs closing is more symbolic than real. Remember, nothing is *forever*.

Not everyone can afford to clear the deck as drastically as one woman did when she sold her house and furniture in one fell swoop and was now furnishing a town house from top to bottom with new furniture. Her actions were regarded with very mixed reactions by her widowed friends. Although some aspects of her move certainly had appeal, not everyone envied her leaving so much behind.

But there are compromises. Whether you choose to live in the same house or apartment or elect to move, your home will feel better as you change things to suit yourself. The old lounge chair your husband sat in and that does not satisfy the contours of your body can be replaced. Colors you fancy can be brought into a room, something new that's visually pleasing is a great uplifter. And just rearranging a room makes one feel revitalized.

Creative Housing Options

Sometimes older women with homes too cumbersome to care for try offering space in exchange for services: "a nice college student" or another widow who will help with the cooking and cleaning—and maybe drive the old Buick that's been sitting in the garage. But advertising for that college student is advertising for a stranger and the idea is soon abandoned or vetoed by the children. As for the widow-companion of old, she's extinct; she is now a professional companion who expects to be paid for services. I receive about 100 calls a month from elderly widows or their children who have "a beautiful home for someone who needs a place" but never have had one inquiry from anyone seeking the bottom half of that arrangement. Under the right conditions renting out a room or a section of a large house, especially to someone you already know, is well worth considering and helps defray expenses.

Younger single women, however, especially those with children, are more successful at joint householding. Where the overriding concerns are those of child-care expenses and lessening burdensome chores, the combined efforts of two single parents is a workable solution. Most often the arrangements are short-term and not intended to be permanent.

Within the past decade, though, women have been experimenting with a number of more stable and creative housing options. Changes in social attitudes and in the policies of lending institutions have made it possible for women to purchase and rent homes jointly. Small complexes—as opposed to large projects—that permit individual privacy but have joint facilities for recreation and entertaining are offered as an alternative for women who want to live together yet apart. Under some arrangements meals are eaten together, sometimes not. Unlike the communes of the '60s, this kind of house sharing is tailored for the more conventional woman. One house I visited had been converted so that there were three master bedrooms, one for each of the three owners—two widows and one divorcee. The kitchen and family room were used in common. The dining room and living room—a combined effort in furnishing and decorating—could be used by any of the three for individual entertaining.

You have many options. You can buy, sell, rent, share or even drive around from place to place in a recreational vehicle. Consider them all, or, perhaps, try them all.

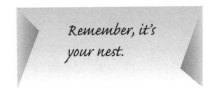

Remember, it's your nest.

Traveling Alone

THE NUMBER-TWO MYTH ABOUT WIDOWS is that they will take a trip, meet a man and remarry. Number one is that an elementary-school beau will magically turn up a widower. It's a logical happy ending if you believe that the only happy ending for a widow is marriage. But if you view widowhood as the beginning of just one more passage in life, there may be 1,001 happy endings that are equal or better, depending on your point of view.

What no widow should immediately do is embark on a trip before she has disposed of the visible ghosts. Well-meaning friends and relatives will advise getting away. Getting away too soon makes returning more difficult. Delay that trip until his pipe no longer sits in the ashtray and his coat no longer hangs in the hall closet.

Visiting Friends and Family

Where most women go for their first solo trip is straight to the comfort of friends and family. Back home or visiting the children is a safe haven with fewer unknowns. It's been done before; he was with you. Unpredictably, though, such visits may or may not be satisfying. Often a visit is consoling; one more needed good-bye. Also, along with the security of being enclosed in caring arms, the woman alone begins to place value on herself as a single human being: "Look, they really love *me,* it's okay if I'm not *us."* One recently widowed woman echoed the sentiments of many when she said that going back to her hometown, being with her family and having them share her tears and memories helped her "lay him to rest."

For others, however, the return-to-the-bosom routine is a disappointment. "I went to visit my in-laws," one businesswoman said on returning from her vacation, "who, after all, loved Charlie as much as I did. It was depressing. We were never really that close. I don't know why I went. I guess I thought I should."

Another older widow recalled, "I went to visit my daughter. It was nice seeing the children and my son-in-law was so sweet. He took off two days so we could go places, but, you know they have their own lives. The next time I won't stay so long; a week would have been enough. I was actually glad to come home to peace and quiet."

New Places

Judging from repeated accounts, after a while visiting the folks at home ceases to satisfy as a steady diet. Even the fainthearted start thinking of doing something a little more courageous. As you know, there are times when the choices seem limited: Sit on your duff and feel safe—or get off your duff and feel scared. Whatever your own level of courage (and finances)—a museum trip with a senior-citizen group, a tour of Europe with an older grandchild, an Elderhostel program with a little education thrown in, a bus tour to see the fall foliage or climbing the Himalayas—a little scared is better than too much safety.

Traveling throughout the United States and Canada, either solo or with a few friends, is a good beginning. You won't encounter language problems and most of us have a friend or relative along the route for a backup. There are some great bus tours and rail trips you can book through senior-citizen groups, bank clubs, museums and alumni associations, as well as through travel agencies. Not to be overlooked are such expedition and "adventure" groups as the Sierra Club, Audubon Society, Smithsonian Institution and so on that arrange exciting and soul-satisfying journeys and seminars. Contrary to what you might think, you do not have to be a young backpacker. You can travel with a llama or a burro to carry your gear and be with other novices as apprehensive as yourself. I went on an unforgettable hiking trip to China, sleeping in Buddhist

> *Traveling throughout the United States and Canada, either solo or with a few friends, is a good beginning.*

monasteries on the trail. The ages of that jolly group ranged from 16 to 66.

You may quite legitimately be like Irene, who each summer visited her mother in Kansas and her daughter in Omaha and spent Christmas and Easter on the same circuit. I once calculated that including air fare, presents and taxis, she could have had one humdinger of a jaunt to Casablanca and back. Although her friends urged her on, Irene declared she had no interest in other places. This was what she and William always did, and maybe someday . . . No other person has an accurate thermometer for judging another person's risk level or curiosity saturation point, I've reluctantly learned.

Looking back, my own first solo trip was not very judicious. It was typical of early widowhood where everything goes wrong, not singly but in threes. In other words, my trip was calamitous. The night for which I had a travel reservation to Oaxaca, Mexico, was overbooked. The hotel for which I had no reservation (it's usually so much more fun that way) could only offer "impossible, señora." Alas, out of 52 available weeks, I had selected the very one the presidential candidate had also selected for campaigning in that state. Every room had been rented or commandeered for his entourage, his family and the members of the press. How I ended up in a room next to a sleazy bar in the market district, with garbage on the floor and a single, unshielded bulb overlooking a bed of questionable history, was funny in the telling months later, but not then. Although I would recommend much more looking before leaping, that experience was a lesson in survival techniques. I am now an absolute authority on how to get a room in Oaxaca.

> *I am now an absolute authority on how to get a room in Oaxaca.*

Tours

Probably safer, and certainly the more customary way to travel if you are alone and going to a foreign country, is an all-arranged tour. Seek out a travel agent who has firsthand experience with the locale and tour company. With a tour, the positive side is that details are taken care of and people look after your comfort and social needs. On the negative side, you do a lot of catering to the wants of others, such as waiting, shopping and touristy sightseeing. It should also be mentioned that although single supplements cost more, taking on a roommate sight unseen may be even more costly.

One unhappy woman, reporting about her trip to Greece, said, "The couples stuck together, and the women travelers also came in twos. The only other unattached, middle-aged woman was the one I was paired with, for reasons of economy, by the company. She filled the nights with snoring and the days with silence. She wore color-coordinated bows in her hair. People avoided the two of us. Fortunately, Greece and all its glory came through."

Best of all, I think, is a tour or cruise that has a focus of interest similar to yours. There are groups for bird-watchers, music lovers, history buffs, needlework fanciers, gourmets, RV enthusiasts, bicyclists and people with like philosophical leanings. There are walking, skiing and hiking trips; solid weeks of golf, fishing, tennis and practically anything else that can be done from a standing or sitting position. You'll find advertisements for these trips in magazines catering to those special interests. These trips can be less expensive and offer a good opportunity for meeting people with whom you have something in common. If the number-two myth doesn't pan out, you will at least have had an enjoyable time and will have met some interesting people.

Travel Alone or with Others?

You can also drive throughout the United States and Canada, although many widows hesitate to undertake this trip on their own. Solo or with a few friends, the highways and byways offer some wonderful vacation opportunities. My greatest pleasure now is driving through the West to the national parks (this is from someone who couldn't even bear to have the radio on when she had to pass a truck, so heavy was her concentration). With good road maps and a carefully checked-out car, many of us find that as our experience level rises our anxiety level plummets. As long as you stay on the main roads, emergency assistance is usually available. You have only to lift the hood of the car and someone will stop to help or call for help for you. In spite of all the stories we hear to the contrary, there are still a lot of good people out there and a driver in distress is usually rescued by a compassionate soul in short time. However, you may be safer if you take the advice of many state highway patrolmen and lock your doors and hold up a sign requesting passing motorists to send assistance from the next gas station. Or invest in a cell phone for emergencies.

Because most of us hesitate to embark on a trip to a foreign country alone, our first choice—and often, we feel, our only choice—is to look for company. That's fine, but don't get trapped into traveling with someone whose interests and tastes (food, sleeping habits, curiosity level) you continually have to accommodate. It's a drag. Also, unless you know them well and love them dearly, do not travel as a third with a couple. Chances are you will feel more lonely and awkward, get caught in their occasional crossfire and feel obliged to do what they want to do rather than what you want to do.

Go it alone if the cost of compromise is too high. You always meet more people and make more friends traveling singly than in twos. That applies as well to the more adventurous person who books her own trip and is her own tour leader. Young, single women have blazed the trail for the older widow, so traveling on your own is acceptable and possible these days. Those who try it return glowing with new confidence and report that the dangers do not exceed those encountered at home. Refer to the box on page 167 for tips on traveling solo.

A final word of advice: Start small and learn about your interests and needs, but keep expanding. Start a file of interesting travel articles and read about faraway places. Investigate the methods of travel, question travel agents, seek out people who have been there. Don't overlook the shelves and shelves of books in your public library. Investigate the discount outlets available for those who can take advantage of last-minute travel opportunities (including those on the Internet) and look for off-season bargains. Think "adventure!" The greater limitation is not finances, but guts.

Tips for Traveling Alone

- When traveling abroad, choose countries where you speak the language so you can talk to as many people as possible.

- Don't carry a pocketbook. Keep your passport and money on your person (a small purse that attaches to a belt is handy) and carry the extras in something like a canvas shopping bag. That's about the best you can do as far as precautionary measures.

- Travel light and with only as much as you can carry yourself. You will be surprised how far one skirt, one pair of slacks and one dress will stretch, especially when you are running for connections.

- Don't hesitate to go to a new and unknown place as long as you are interested in the sights or history and have some plan for their viewing. Good guidebooks are a must and local sight-seeing trips are a big help.

- While a woman alone is apt to feel uncomfortable dining in a classy restaurant in the evening, you can have great lunches with no problem. Most of the time you will get first-class service in the evening, as well. Just call in advance, say you will be alone and ask if they can serve you. Reserve the late evenings for recording your day's activities and thoughts and for planning for the day ahead. It keeps you off the streets and is not bad at all if you've had a full day.

- When in a foreign place, don't sit around the hotel lobby or in your room during the daytime. Get out, talk to people, share a table in a cafe, take local bus rides. If you are afraid of getting lost, go to the end of the line and back. Get maps of the city and walk. A good way to meet another unattached traveler and a possible dinner companion is to take one of those city sight-seeing buses. Be a conversation starter. Always pay your own way.

- Take along a camera. You never feel awkward or shy as long as you are taking a picture or looking as though you might take a picture.

- Don't feel sorry for yourself when you see happy couples. Head for a sidewalk cafe, have a cup of coffee, watch the world go by and think, "Wow, look at me!" Be flexible. If plans don't work out, your train doesn't run or some such disaster occurs, consider it a challenge for creative substituting. If it rains on your walking day see a local movie in any language, observe how the courts are run, or shop for a raincoat.

- Avoid typical couples-type places such as beach-resort hotels or condominium vacation havens. Besides being frequented by families and couples who have their own built-in amusements, these spots usually have little more than view and climate to keep you occupied. They are not guide-book places.

It Wasn't Perfect All the Time

WIDOWS COME IN ALL SIZES and so do their tears. Not every marriage is made in heaven, and in every marriage right here on earth there are good days and bad days. But, just as few widows reminisce about quarrels and unhappiness, few crow about their liberation.

In all my contacts with widows I've known only two who had no tears and said so quite honestly. One, impatient with the disconsolate outpourings of others with whom she was having lunch, complained, "Hey, aren't any of you glad to be free? My husband never wanted to do anything; this is my opportunity—finally—to live."

The other, after attending two meetings of a widows' support group, said that she was "in the wrong place. I didn't have it good like all of you, and I don't miss him. We used to fight all the time. I'm thankful it's over." Both times these remarks were greeted with uncomfortable silence by the other women. Surely, all had some small measure of identification with what those women were saying. It wasn't all halos and golden wings; everyone knew what those women were talking about.

> *To a fault, widows raise their spouses to sainthood.*

Did you never play with thoughts of being free to roam, having fewer responsibilities, no bickering, no quibbling and no sulking? Can't you recall a day when you wanted to drop a potted palm from the roof just to relieve the monotony? How about wanting to scream if you heard that story one more time or ate in that same unexciting restaurant because they didn't "specialize in heartburns"? Did you never rein your words and deeds to "avoid a fuss" and "keep the peace"? It *wasn't* perfect.

To a fault, widows raise their spouses to sainthood. As one man said following his marriage to a widow, "I never knew of a perfect man until I heard about my wife's first husband." As the days pass, all the annoying habits, solid disagreements and nagging resentments that can—and do—dot any marriage become a blur. Through the filter of absence, it was "a perfect marriage" and "we were a very close couple." Try recalling some of your husband's aggravating quirks. It's very hard. Only reluctantly do we remember the man who never put his dirty socks in the hamper, never heard of a social engagement until an hour before departure, occupied the bathroom longer than was humanly possible. "And never told me anything about our finances," would rather stay home than go out whenever there was a good movie playing, gave dirty looks across the bridge table, ate anything you put in front of him as long as it was on time. Plus, he always walked out of the room rather than discuss a problem.

We forget we were married to men who snored at night, awoke in the morning feeling out of sorts, made love distractedly and, in short, were human.

That's hardly strange. Even when an individual has endured what looks to us a miserable alliance—a pathological pairing—the surviving spouse will disintegrate in profound grief. (I knew a couple who played two-handed pinochle with the bread knife placed on the table between them; they never spoke to each other except to argue. Still, when her husband died, the widow never rebounded from her grieving.) The range of joy in some marriages goes from mediocre to *more* mediocre. Yet the surviving spouse is more grieved than freed. For the generations of the '30s and '40s, the divorce option was not easily exercised; people stayed married and I suppose, like mother's cooking, it's the old story of loving what you get used to.

But supposing you do look back at those funny—and not so funny—parts of your marriage that were negative: likes you didn't share, dislikes you didn't agree with, the tyranny of time and duties. Is that disloyal? Sinful?

Women who have spent years taking care of an invalid mate talk about how happy they were to have had him all those years. Only in passing do they mention something that indicates the negative aspects of that arrangement, that they have few friends now because they infrequently socialized with others during that long period of illness.

> *Try recalling some of your husband's aggravating quirks. It's very hard.*

"I never made the decisions," "He didn't tell me about those things," and "He wasn't a person you could argue with" portray the very model of the one-speaker-one-timid-listener couple. What is omitted from the "but we were very happy" that follows is that happiness depended on strict adherence to long-ago established rules and roles. Everything was perfect as long as the compliant mate never changed.

"I always thought I was too dumb to learn about money" implies and *so did he.*

"He was a very stubborn man" means that what he said went, and reveals just a whisper of discontent.

Sometimes, a widow will confess through her tears, as though she had committed a crime, that she had started to file for a divorce before her husband died. "I was so mad at him because after he retired he wouldn't go anyplace or do anything but sit around the house; I thought it would bring him to his senses." Now she is harvesting the past for the good memories and coming up with a bumper crop. If she made her little confession within the hearing of a few dozen other widows she would probably hear another meek little voice admitting "Me, too"—and another, and another.

Loss Is Complicated

The ambivalence we have in the sorrow of loss lies buried and tucked away in human nature. There is nothing wicked in admitting a sense of relief that a long, imprisoning illness is over not only "for him" but also "for me." It is healthy for a man or woman to feel a stirring of hope about what might be ahead for him or her: more fulfilling sex life, days without the apprehension of conflict, greater freedom, independence. It is permissible to note some of the less praiseworthy characteristics of your spouse. And you might even take heart when you catalogue a dozen or so of the compromises that kept you "a happy couple." Granted, you might gladly do it all over again. But now that you have—and not of your own choosing— become one person, you might just as well temper the so-called *perfection of the past* and give the present a chance.

I'm often amused when I witness a couple going through some of the old rituals once so familiar to me. It's hard to keep a straight face when I hear the man, after studying the restaurant menu at length, ask his wife, "What do you think I should order?" Or how about the conversation about the best route to the Johnsons', "Should I take Broadway or Main?"—usually good for 15 minutes of spirited discussion. Once, when I was driving up the coast of Oregon by myself I tried to conjure up the dialogue I was missing had my husband been sharing the beauty and adventure of the trip. All I could invent was "Just look at that, isn't it incredible?" Oh, and not to be remiss, I recalled the great two-way conversation that goes: "Hungry?" "I don't know, are you?"

There may be envy lurking in my bones, but at times like that I am better able to relish my unencumbered single-hood. I've noticed that a little reality goes a long way toward restoring a balance between the poor me and the new me. I hear other single women voice the same

> *It is permissible to note some of the less praiseworthy characteristics of your spouse.*

mixed emotions should we decide to go out for dinner after a meeting: "Sure, I don't have to be home at any special time." They will remark on couples in restaurants who sit without speaking one word to each other—talked out—and they now hear shadings of male chauvinism in remarks that once they accepted as gospel. And what widow doesn't smile inwardly when she hears Mr. and Mrs. Bicker split hairs? "It was last Monday." "No, dear," the other corrects with great patience, "Remember? It was Tuesday." It sounds so funny now—like ancient history.

Sure you had a wonderful husband, certainly yours was an extraordinary marriage, but it wasn't always perfect—so perfect that the future holds nothing worth the search. Sometimes people will get to talking about how they have changed since becoming widowed and shake their heads in wonder that anything good could have resulted from their loss. They are different now, they say. It's hard to explain. They were happy before and wish with all their hearts it was still the same, they say. Every relationship has its costs and they were happy to pay the price. But as one incredulous woman, a widow of only a year, clearly stated, "You know, as much as I loved my husband I could not marry him today—not since I found that I have a mind of my own. And if he came back and saw *me* today he'd run back after 24 hours."

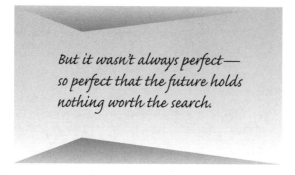

*But it wasn't always perfect—
so perfect that the future holds
nothing worth the search.*

On a Scale of 1 to 10, What Am I Without a Man?

MANY OF US WERE RAISED on the lore that behind every great man there is a woman—lucky gal. We gained status through our husbands: The wife of a brain surgeon was two points above the wife of an assembly-line worker. We saw ourselves through the eyes of a man and acted accordingly. For a woman to feel beautiful, worthwhile and secure, she needs a man. True?

Widows have to examine that credo. When asked how they have changed, women who have coped with widowhood say they are more assertive, feel more capable, more challenged, and enjoy being independent. As one woman phrased it, "I like being right for a change." Women say they are more social, have a wider acquaintanceship and are more curious about exploring new interests. A growing number of widows also say they do not wish to remarry or "take care of a man again."

Given all those positive responses why, oh why, do widows still place themselves on the negative side of the ledger if they are without a man? When a widow reports she is dating or getting married, the congratulations are glowing. The widows congratulating her, though, fight down a secret knot of envy and a feeling of rejection. As daughters we were not taught to be widows and as widows we do not often hear love songs that regale the hymn to self and the joy of accomplishment.

> *Women say they are more social, have a wider acquaintanceship and are more curious about exploring new interests.*

I wish it were not so, but we do think of life in absolute terms: the opposite of having someone is having no one. In this mood widows say they are lonely, outside the normal circle, feel unloved and purposeless, forgetting that they have known the same sad thoughts since the age of five—with or without a man.

I think congratulations are equally deserved when a widow reports that she has written her first check, driven her first mile or made her first solo decision. Let us applaud when she goes to a movie, restaurant or party on her own (if she so wishes), appreciates her own company, can experience the difference between loneliness and solitude, and takes pleasure in her solitude. She is a smashing success when she is loving, giving and caring as she ever was. She even loves herself when she discovers she has a mind, opinions and untapped resources. I think she has reached a milestone when she can be celibate without sacrificing her sexuality and sexual without compromising her independence. Cheers when she has good friends whom she can do things with and be with.

Not for all the world would I put down marriage; it's wonderful, and better still when both partners are independent, happy people. But it's not for everyone; joining up with a man is not necessarily better than living without one. We are all winners when we are self-reliant and satisfied with ourselves—when *selfhood* takes the place of *widowhood*.

So, what am I without a man? Ten, not zero.

> *She has reached a milestone when she can be celibate without sacrificing her sexuality and sexual without compromising her independence.*

Looking Back to Say Good-bye

A Journal Entry

Dear Martin,

People and things have certainly changed in these past ten years. Me, for one thing. While you have remained young-looking and handsome, I look quite a bit older: more flab, flaps, creaks and what you used to call *character lines*. Quite a lot of character.

Outside the weather is colder; inside the bills are higher, and all around us the world is crazier. The Marines no longer just sing about the halls of Montezuma to the shores of Tripoli, they go there. A Republican has been in the White House for two terms and I can just hear what you would have said to that.

Big changes in our house, too. You won't believe it, but the bed gets made only once a week, and all those papers I used to move to your desk with a loud and meaningful sigh don't even make it to the desk—any flat surface will do. You'd love it, total disorder. But the shower no longer drips, the driveway has been paved and the check stubs now get filled in. I fixed the shower myself, got five estimates for the driveway (stayed up two weeks deciding) and have a ledger system for keeping accounts. In the past 12 months the checkbook balanced twice, a 200-percent improvement. Can you believe it?

You also won't believe that I drive mountain roads, speak before an audience at the drop of a hat, am involved in many community organizations and serve as the director of one. We both thought that was your area. Of course, I still have trouble with north and south, percentages (see above), heavy boxes and cold feet—to name a few.

This past holiday season I had my annual open-house party for 50 people—many of them the friends and couples we used to socialize with. It's become a real event; keeps me in touch and takes care of social obligations. I get so busy I don't know Christmas Eve from New Year's Eve.

Our son was a little miffed when, a few years ago, I first declined his invitation to spend the holidays with his family and worked out my own patterns. But recently he told me how proud he is of me and the life I have made for myself. We both cried.

And that's another thing. As a family we have become very close and able to talk freely with each other. Until you died we all "spared" each other, but now we know that sparing and sharing are more than a letter apart. Sometimes when we are watching the grandchildren you have never seen, your son says, "Dad would get such a charge out of them." A tear may roll down his cheek, unattended, and your daughter-in-law and I join in. It's sad but wonderfully comforting.

A new year is unfolding, the calendar is filled with plans. There are days to look forward to, and some I could do without. I wish you were here, but were you to return you would not find me the same person, and I don't think I could go back to being that person. But you know, I believe you'd like this one too.

Love,

Me

Part 4

Besides Which

THIS SECTION IS FOR YOUNG WIDOWS, WIDOWERS and those who are concerned about widows. Though addressed to them more specifically, these chapters are connected to the preceding sections by the common thread of widowhood and of course, grief. They amplify and expand what young widows, widowers and families have been reading here.

Young widows, and there are approximately 400,000 under the age of 45, feel apart and singular; they only rarely encounter each other. And widowers, although they number more than three million, also stand alone—bravely. For the adult children of a widowed parent this is a confusing time of adjustment to a new relationship with a new person; widowhood changes everyone.

For all of them the following chapters are intended to dispel ancient myths and clear the way for living again.

Young Widows

FOR YOUNG WIDOWS *nothing is fair.* Today's bride is more prepared for divorce than widowhood—as is everyone else. Her position seems so tragic and unnatural that people refer to her not as just "a widow." They feel obliged to add an explanation: "the young woman whose husband died of cancer" or "was killed in a car accident."

"Betrayed by fate" was the way one woman put it when her husband was fatally injured while riding his bike to have his Ph.D. dissertation photocopied. "He had all those doors to open. Why in hell did he open the wrong one?" Behind one of those doors was her own delayed career as well as their never-to-be plans. She was angry. Although her friends were loyally attentive after the tragedy she, nevertheless, felt isolated and cheated. They were all couples and she knew no other 32-year-old widow. At her age that was not supposed to happen.

Not that facing the death of a spouse is ever easy, but a young widow has truly received a hard blow. Bad enough that she is left with much more unfinished business and many more unfulfilled plans than someone married for a longer time. More often none of her lifetime experiences have cushioned her for coping with this premature death. So while she goes through the same stages and phases and private agony we talk about throughout this book, she is, in addition, more unprepared for what has happened and what to expect.

Unlike the older widow, it never entered her mind. It was not statistically scheduled to happen—although in actual numbers there are about 400,000 widows under the age of 45. And also unlike the older widow, this may be her first actual brush with death. She may never have even attended a funeral, and her parents, siblings and peers are all alive. Nevertheless, she is thrust into the pragmatic—and frightening—details and decisions of funeral and burial, devoid of the shock absorber of past experiences. In that case, her first impulse may be a strong desire to run away, for which she feels guilty and ashamed. Should her parents or in-laws take over, as so often happens, she ends up feeling helpless and even less in control of her life. There is no winning script.

Higher Expectations

Nevertheless, she is supposed to be resilient, to adjust and handle problems in double time because she's young. "You're young, you'll marry again," the older folk predict, which seems like the final insult: Great! You get another chance. Her peers also don't see it from her perspective. To them one loss is very much like another: "Look at Suzie, divorced less than a year and she's back in school, dating and down to 110 pounds. But Sally (whose husband had a fatal heart attack at 37) is still dabbing at her eyes with damp tissues and flying off the handle if you try to give her—all 160 pounds of her— some good advice."

> *When there are young children, she notices for the first time how many activities need a father.*

The difference is that Suzie has lots of divorced, new friends with whom to review the past and plan optimistically for the future. Sally's old and only friends give her a not-again look if she speaks of her past, and her future doesn't exist—yet. Also, a widow, young or old, does *not* shed her grief like a snake's skin and add a B.S. degree to her name, is not overly conscious about her looks and doesn't want to get it over and done with.

For her, the transition to a new identity is a slower and more halting process. So, impatient friends tend to drift away once the newness of tragedy is past, leaving her isolated and without a cheering squad. The reason wartime widows cope so much better is because they have that cheering squad of not only friends but whole communities, as well as the knowledge of each other.

Understandable Anger

No wonder then, that a young widow has a higher level of anger. Who can blame her? Looking about, she sees her friends going off to concerts and ski weekends as before, her dreams for a family, house and security wiped out. When there are young children, she notices for the first time how many activities need a father. As a widow-mother she feels trapped and cheated, but must go on as before.

Although her anger can be a healthy, positive force, it is at times hostile, close to the surface and not well tolerated by friends and family. Like a strong wind in a storm, her rage can be a force for discharging her emotions. She is less likely to become bogged down in the depression and martyrdom caused by suppressing her angry feelings. She may lash out—for no sound reason—at anyone handy.

I once listened to a young widow deliver a 30-minute tirade against old friends, blaming them for failing to take her son fishing and camping over the summer. Although the child had never in the past participated in those particular activities, the woman thought she was being perfectly logical as she pointed out, over and over, "They know Barry has no father now." Reasonable, no. Typical, yes. It is understandable that friends, after being subjected to a tongue-lashing or two, or the more passive-aggressive reaction of glaring silence, will throw up their hands and say, "I've tried, but she's impossible." I personally wish those friends would hang in there a while and tolerate a few temper tantrums—and take Barry camping.

Parents

In contrast, mothers and fathers tend to be overly protective. In an automatic parental reflex, they regress to earlier instincts and want "to make it all better." Standing by helplessly is not what parents do well and becoming helpless is not what works well for the daughter. Young widows say the love and solicitude that is so welcome during the first months can become a bind later on. Suddenly, they realize, they have been taken over.

When George was alive Sally's parents refrained from telling her how to budget, how unhealthy a dinner of pizza and Coke is, how many hours of sleep a five-year-old needs, and how many months of grieving is normal. Now, every Sunday morning, unconstrained, they phone and tell. Sally, instead of casually shrugging them off as she had learned to do, feels as criticized and inadequate as when she was an adolescent. How, in the name of love, she wonders, can she accept the gift of their help and sympathy without the strings they're wrapped in? One suggestion might be for Mom and Dad to recall how she learned to ride a bike—one driver—as they stood by and watched.

In-Laws

Next in the problem line, young widows say, are the in-laws. In-laws may actually be the most prevailing problem for young widows because that is what they talk about most

> *The in-laws are one of the widow's strongest links to her husband; the tensions are tight and prickly.*

among themselves. The headaches of that particular relationship are universal even during marriage and in widowhood they are even more so. The widow and her children are the last living breath of the son or brother who died. The in-laws are one of the widow's strongest links to her husband; the tensions are tight and prickly.

Young widows say they are bound by a strong sense of loyalty to his parents and siblings and resent the restraints that obligation so often imposes upon them: Sunday dinners, making certain the children phone Grandma, misspent vacations together, what to do about *his* picture on the bureau. Both sides are aware that what may be good for one may be bad for the other; dating, marriage, relocating and just plain letting go are some of the things that threaten the symmetry of this relationship. Not to forget, also, that the husband was the one in charge of running interference. Communications that may not have been too forthright to begin with can stagnate even further now.

One complaint these widows echo over and over: "I don't know what my mother-in-law wants. She says 'Never mind' and 'Don't bother' anytime I invite them, and when they do visit, they drive me crazy because they're so afraid they're interfering—which they are.

We're all walking on eggs." Solution: Could everybody—widow, parents, and in-laws—please say what they mean? A satisfying relationship is not built on eggs.

On the good-news side of the ledger is that both parents and in-laws can be a tremendous help and usually want to be. For the widow that may mean setting her own meaningful boundaries and sometimes turning away from a very tempting offer: Hawaii during the school term, a fabulous restaurant dinner with a two-year-old, short-term peace for a little white lie, and an honest answer in place of "It doesn't matter" and "Whatever you like."

For the in-laws it may be that they see their daughter-in-law not as an unreliable bequest from their son, but just as a person who needs to become yet another person.

Money Issues

What else plagues the young widow? Money, of course. Young couples getting started don't ordinarily have much money in the bank and many placed life insurance on the back burner. For the widow with children under 18 and managing on Social Security, there are few luxuries even when she supplements that income.

Returning to work or looking for a job too soon after the death of a spouse may, in many cases, be essential. But work should not become the sole end product. Some of the widows who have tried blocking out their grief by pushing themselves into a demanding job advise against it. They describe their days to be a series of getting up, going to work, coming home and getting up again. No time-out for the thinking, feeling, talking, making friends and striving for change. Instead, depression, health problems, family breakdowns and all kinds of sneaky disturbances make their way to the surface, unannounced, in protest. Be aware that all work and keeping busy to avoid feelings can result in a rut effect that reaches from zero to zero—spanning nothing.

Intimacy Issues

If work and grieving don't always mix well, sex and grieving mix less well. A common reaction to early widowhood is: What am I going to do with the rest of my sex life? It's not so unusual or shocking for a young widow, while still numb and very much in mourning, to have a passionate sexual encounter that "just happened." Sex is as much an emotional release as screaming or crying, and emotions are in quite a jumble at this time. Further along the way, some women say they are preoccupied with wondering whether they will be attractive to men, be able to sleep with another man, and are still sexually alive. Some just wonder, and some test it out. One woman, for no reason she ever could understand, acquired three lovers at the same time, about six months after her husband's death. She didn't really desire or enjoy the sex; still, it was some time before she ended the affairs.

More typically, young widows say they do not feel ready for intimacies with another man for a long while—some for as long as two years. For some women, job, career and children get a higher priority than sex. How a young woman regarded sex and herself as a sexual being before becoming widowed will largely influence her attitudes and behavior now. Regardless, she should not expect herself to awaken one morning feeling sexually whole, willing and able to take on emotional risks and make only wise decisions about new partners. It's still a process of ups and downs.

Comforting the Children

Widows ask how to deal with their young children's bereavement. They are the helpless parents here. Child specialists agree that children should

> *Child specialists agree that children should not be protected from the knowledge of death.*

not be protected from the knowledge of death. Unless one has a strong religious conviction to the contrary they should not be told that Daddy goes to heaven. No child can find that an acceptable concept—if it ever was. A child should know about death as and when it has meaning for him. His questions should be answered honestly and his father's absence talked about.

When a child cries that he wants his father, his mother can only say, "I would like him here, too." If he never speaks of his father, his mother should not acquiesce to that silence with her own silence or consistently hide her tears. Talk! Equally, mothers have to avoid turning the child into a constant companion and confidant—a comforting temptation for the lonely young widow. Even a 6-year-old has his own life to live. So much is basic.

> *When a child cries that he wants his father, his mother can only say, "I would like him here, too."*

A great deal goes on in little heads; patient and careful listening cannot be overemphasized. Children have concrete concepts and take literally words like *lost, return,* and *watching you.* After attending a picnic for widows with children under 12, one 8-year-old was relieved to meet another girl whose father was also "lost." She admitted to her mother that, "In school I always say my parents are divorced, because I thought we were the only ones who couldn't find ours."

The fatherless child may initially feel more deprived, abandoned or fearful that his mother might also die. He needs to express his distress. Talking about it with his surviving parent is still the best of all therapies. It may take time and patience. If the child senses that the subject is disturbing for his mother or other family members, he soon learns to keep his thoughts to himself. On the other hand, he need not be pitied. Pity carries a message of incompetence, it's a put-down. There is plenty of evidence to prove that single parents are good child-rearers and that a child does not suffer psychological trauma because there is no father or mother in the home.

> *A great deal goes on in little heads; patient and careful listening cannot be overemphasized.*

Coping with Grief

People ask whether younger widows, logically, shouldn't make a better accommodation to loss because their sense of self is more intact. We assume that women over 50 suffer a greater identity crisis because their generation has so much more invested in the role of wife and mother. How people cope through grief and the duration of profound grieving is not related to age as much as to each individual's ability to grow and meet change. I knew an 85-year-old widow who subtracted 15 years from her age when she registered in a summer college program "to avoid fuss" and a 22-year-old widow who sat in her apartment day in and day out watching television. Young widows believe their role identity of wife and mother is a feminine characteristic that has not changed in spite of social changes, careers and financial independence. And as if to prove their contention, they use the same words as older widows, *alone, freakish* and *outsider,* in describing their relationship with their world.

My own observation is that, in general, younger widows do not reach a plateau in grieving where they are as accepting of the status quo as are some older women. Once they get started, they envision greater potential for themselves. Forty-nine percent of under-45 widows will remarry, but the other 51 percent do not appear to be twiddling their thumbs. In all the discussions I've witnessed, sooner or later the talk drifts beyond in-laws, parents and children to "going back to nursing," "starting a business," "taking children into my home," "becoming a social worker" and even "building a tract of 40 houses."

If there is an end to grieving, its beginning lies here, in giving up some of the past and looking toward the future, making new plans, making new friends and "leaving yourself open." In any case, it may be reassuring to know that young widows have a wonderful capacity to emerge, saying that, yes, it *was* unfair, but they are tougher and stronger now.

> *If there is an end to grieving, its beginning lies here, in giving up some of the past and looking toward the future.*

And Widowers, Too

WHEN MEN AND WOMEN SIT DOWN TOGETHER to talk about themselves after becoming widowed, they are struck by the sameness of what they are experiencing—and then—the unsameness. In the beginning, widows and widowers share the same emotional crisis: Both are equally bereft, confused, lost and brokenhearted. Both have lost part of themselves; they are as shattered. On this both men and women agree.

They smile and shake hands at the funeral with the same "out of it" expression, they are equally prone to anger at being left. They upbraid themselves with "if onlys" and are correspondingly subject to depression and the rest of the assorted reactions in the grief repertoire. The same kind of foolish inner dialogues take place in the male head as in the female's: "My daughter would have been much better off if her mother were here instead of me," or "Dolly was always the life of the party; no one wants a dud like me around."

In becoming uncoupled, the interdependencies that made an alliance click suddenly appear as individual flaws. That big, strong guy may unexpectedly feel as helpless as a baby on his own, just as the totally in-charge woman might learn she is afraid to be alone at night. A major component of bereavement is the ungluing of the ego, the half-person syndrome. "I'm no one special anymore." And that's widowhood, not gender.

Nevertheless, there are differences. Although they are not related to the y-chromosome, they are so deeply imbedded in our social mores and customs as to be absolute male traits. Strength and bravery, for instance. From the widower's point of view, his is a tough act. Men may appear to bear up better than women, but their phony front is the result of generations of hard practice rather than authentic toughness and is no shield from true grief. They envy women their tears. Although at present we grant men permission to cry, they don't believe it. Too many people still react from out of the past: They squirm, look at their feet and lose their tongues when a man weeps from the heart. So men hold back. One man described how embarrassed he felt the first day back at work when he lost his self-control and sobbed as he read the sympathy card on his desk from his fellow workers. "They were all sympathetic, I'm sure," he said, "but no one put his arms around me the way they would have a woman. Crazy as it was, I wanted to be held—like a little kid."

Also, widowers are expected "to recover" sooner than women. After a few months of stocking the freezer and giving instructions on how to work the washing machine, families express concern if Dad hasn't resumed full semblance of his past life. "You have to get out more, Dad. It's time," the children say. For a man, "getting on with it" unrealistically presumes that he is "getting over it" without relapses—never "sliding backward."

Long before he is ready, when his emotions are still silently overflowing and he has an almost compulsive wish to talk about his wife, her illness, her courage, how she drove better than a truck driver and could make anything grow, the widower's friends invite him to meet an eligible woman. His buddies thump him on the shoulder and invite him to have a beer and watch the game instead of making opportunities for reactions and memories. Single women make overtures that awaken no response in him—and even strike terror in his heart—and he wonders if that is normal and if he is. Moreover, he has no one to talk it over with; she's gone.

As with the other myths about maleness, it is also supposed that what every man needs is "a woman to take care of him." To which many men reply, "Not since frozen entrees and machine-made socks they don't." They may not care to, but they already know or can learn how to cook, vacuum and do laundry; labor-saving equipment has made this an equal-opportunity country in that regard. In fact, many widowed

What is missing, though, is the living energy of the person who turned the house into a home; the one who was, in so many ways, the foundation.

men tenderly cared for their wives at home during a long, terminal illness; they cooked, cleaned, nursed her and seldom left her alone. Men confirm that, at worst, home duties are learnable even if it means frying a pork chop and cooking instant mashed potatoes seven nights a week for a while. While there is a fringe of single men who eat all their meals in restaurants and are hopelessly helpless, the average widower feels maligned by the man-burns-water image. What men miss least of all, they say, is dinner on the table and clean sheets on the bed.

What is missing, though, is the living energy of the person who turned the house into a home; the one who was, in so many ways, the foundation. "The house was her territory, it was hers. Without her in it I feel like a stranger," one older man said sadly. Indeed, very little had been changed or moved since his wife died. It was still hers although he now cooked his own meals and someone came in to vacuum once a week.

Loneliness

Ask a man what is the worst, and the answer is the same: "Loneliness." On a loneliness scale men would probably rate higher than women by several marks because they cope with bereavement less openly, keeping their feelings masked and, sometimes, not being able to open up even to themselves. Women have other women to talk to. Men don't. Women have girlfriends, men have buddies, and with buddies there are more don'ts than do's. Drop two women on a desert isle and within the first hour they will have exchanged the story of their lives, while two men in the same time will have gotten as far as where they lived and what they did for a living. Widows have networks and other women to lean on to help get them through grief. Widowers have clubs, unions and Monday-night bowling; slap-on-the-back groups.

To his further disadvantage, the average over-50 North American male comes complete with a '50s morality that sticks to him like flypaper. At a time when he needs friends—not sex—and a listening ear—not bull—he finds no one to turn to. Most men will tell you, no matter how lonely both may be, one man does *not* phone another single man for dinner and a movie. Why? "What would he think?" is the answer. Lunch is okay, but never dinner.

We try to analyze the reasoning, but men are helpless to explain the logic—or illogic. One widower's support group came up with the following assortment of two-man social behavior:

- Fishing is fine, but not the theater. No real man will ask another man if he'd like to see a hit musical.
- For any sporting event or golf, tennis and bowling, calling on a man for companionship is in good taste, but never for a church social, a walk in the park or a shopping trip.
- Need a new suit? Don't ask another man to help you choose. "You do that with women."
- Want a poker game? Call the boys. But bridge? "Are you kidding? Not since college, when we couldn't leave the dorm."
- With the guys you have a few beers, a cup of coffee and horse around, talk business and politics, but you don't spill out your guts. Women are more understanding about those things.

When pressed about the question of homosexuality—which seems like the obvious issue behind these rules—men say they're not concerned about being mistaken for a homosexual. They do agree that the constrictions they observe are based on what other people will think of them and what prevails as acceptable male behavior within their social circle. Absurd, they admit, but being seen in certain situations, at certain hours of the day, in the company of one other man makes them squirm just thinking about it. Widowers get married. Sexual needs aside, men seek the company of women for social and emotional survival. Without them, they become hermits.

With most couples, it is the woman who plans the dinner parties, invites the guests, accepts the invitations, orders the tickets and arranges for the couple's social life. She is the social animal; she remembers birthdays and marks special events. Most men are not in charge of parties and weddings and typically pay little attention to their social calendar. Hence, men, suddenly on their own, don't reach for the phone in the middle of the week to plan for the weekend, even when they have the social bank from which to draw. "Are you busy

They also need interim time before adjusting to a new mate in what should be a new life.

Saturday night—want to do something?" is not a male-to-male question. Adding the loss of his "social secretary" to the self-imposed rules of conventional male behavior, the widower seems to be left with only two choices: date or stay home.

Relationship Readiness

Not a bad choice, some say, and here is where the balance shifts in the men's favor. And, if the figures are correct, it is hardly a choice at all, it's a landslide decision. Widowers date and remarry. On the average widowers remarry within two years; widows closer to five. Men are finding that the bonus for surviving is their limited supply. U.S. Census Bureau figures show at ages 55 to 64, more than 80 percent of all men are married compared with 70 percent of women. Then, at ages 65 to 74, the number of men who are married increases to 81 percent, while women drop to 50 percent. And that does not include the large number of couples who are living together but not counted as married. No longer is the older man on the shelf; he is in demand. For men there is a surfeit of women; even the shyest, the shortest and the most timid stand tall in the saddle.

But it's not all easy. Obviously there are pitfalls and problems, the first one being a matter of readiness. Courted by the large field of unmarried, divorced and widowed women, new widowers too often don't take the time to reconstitute themselves. Men do not suffer the loss of identity that women do when their husbands die. Their self-image is not primarily as "Mary's husband" or the "doctor's husband." Nevertheless, they also need interim time before adjusting to a new mate in what should be a new life. Change, challenge, new directions—and all those good things—come slowly by working through grief, not covering it over.

How long does it take? Of course no one can say for sure, and men no more than women "recover." In general, men pick up their lives sooner than do women. One factor, of course, is their numerical advantage. Men also experience an earlier return of sexual interest and some have a sense of exhilaration at having outwitted the general statistics that forecast their earlier demise.

Widows have an inner sense about when they are ready to date or make lifestyle changes, but with widowers the timing is less certain. It's a touchy matter, because, for a man, dating may very well be part of his reconstitution, putting himself back together. Not having other widowers and men friends as part of his social network (for dinner and the movies) with whom he can share his grief as well as his loneliness, most men, of necessity, look for female companionship. Understanding the difference between courtship and friendship can be tricky at a time when either one or the other of the couple is vulnerable and still confused.

> *Understanding the difference between courtship and friendship can be tricky at a time when either one or the other of the couple is vulnerable and still confused.*

Readiness is, unfortunately, too often determined by the wisdom of hindsight. From the delayed insights of some widowers who felt their marriages were all too hasty can be heard: "I guess I wanted a replacement more than a wife. We were living in my house, and I felt resentful if she changed one stick of furniture or wanted to replace the pillows my wife had embroidered, or even a burned pot. We were both miserable." And: "I became impotent when I remarried; she wanted everything different. I realize now it was just too soon." These men were obviously not ready for a new relationship. Any marriage will go awry when one or the other carries too much baggage from the past.

There are also conflicts that arise from the untested assumptions so typical of a hasty courtship. Regarding finances: "I thought we would split the present bills 50-50; we had a prenuptial agreement for our wills, but she wouldn't part with a cent for food or anything. I was going broke; she was getting rich."

Regarding lifestyle: "We met on a cruise, and I thought she liked to travel. But as soon as we made it legal all she wanted to do was stay home and watch TV." And the most disheartening, regarding family relations: "My daughter never liked her. I thought that would change after we married, but I can't get the two together. It's terrible."

Any man—and this applies to women, too—who thinks, while

he is in a rosy cloud of romance, that his children and family will all live in happy harmony with his new wife is not seeing the whole picture. The family may be reacting to more than the woman herself. They may believe the marriage premature—not respectful of the deceased. Or, as often happens, they may be concerned about their own financial position and how the marriage will affect them in any number of ways. In such cases, everyone might do well to consider outside intervention with counselor or clergy and to take the time to try to understand each other before, rather than after, the ceremony.

Despite the stories about men being unmercifully pursued, some widowers, especially those who never had a wide circle of friends, will remain alone and isolated after the death of their wives. Unless he makes himself available and visible, a widower will not find himself in the company of women. It takes a real effort, then, to get out and join the kind of group or activity that attracts men and women with matching interests. The rest is easier than he thinks, but that first push can be frightening to a man who has been out of the dating scene for many years. People may tell him about singles groups, hobby activities and travel clubs. It may be that all he needs is clean fingernails and a pleasant smile, but he is bound to have anxieties and excuses. Especially, he will be anxious about his sexual ability with a new partner. And for the man whose sex life was put on hold by his wife's illness or disinterest—or his own, for that matter—there will be a risk of failure and embarrassment. Also, some men say that they are put off when women are "bold" and they find their advances more threatening than stimulating. It should be noted that arrangements between older couples can be, by mutual consent, satisfying although nonsexual.

> *Unless he makes himself available and visible, a widower will not find himself in the company of women.*

Sexwise, things have changed drastically since the '50s. Men and women in their mid years and later years are talking—and some for the first time—about what's going on with their bodies and souls. Sex is better. Although they are often as jittery about first encounters as when they were teenagers—clammy hands, increased pulse rates, self-doubts and all the rest—in the present climate older couples feel freer. They live together quite openly, sometimes more to the disapproval of their children than their peers, but marriage is still the popular success story. Among widowers and widows it's hard to say which sex benefits more from marriage; each claim it's the other. Men say things like "She wanted three things: the ring, someone to take care of her and someone to squire her around." Women claim that men can't live alone and want someone to keep the house clean and the bed warm. More women than men say they are disinclined to marry again and "to take care of a man." If the ratio of widows to widowers were equal, the question might be honestly resolved. At present, it certainly is true that the percentage of men who recouple is far greater and the duration of their widowhood is shorter. Whether men could live alone and make the adjustment that widows do—well—as one man said, "Thank God I don't have to." To which the majority of men say, "Amen."

Among widowers and widows it's hard to say which sex benefits more from marriage; each claim it's the other.

Notes to the Children

ADULT CHILDREN QUESTION WHAT THEY SHOULD DO for their mother—or father—and how much they should do when one or the other dies. I'm assuming that the prototypes of the son in Alaska who hasn't written in five years and the daughter who, conversely, calls every day for help in solving a personal emergency are not reading this book and that we are talking to the children who, if anything, care too much about their parent.

Most families live through the early months of mourning more by instinct than design and do very well by each other. Later, when family members return to their own lives, is the time when pieces fall out of the puzzle and the children feel the strains of their new role and wonder how to fulfill it. Unfamiliar with death themselves and bereft of a parent who, until now, may have been a significant source of their own emotional support, the children have neither the experience nor preparation for dealing with a widowed parent.

With the elderly surviving parent, the natural tendency is to take over, because adult children have already, to some extent, moved into the positions of counselor and adviser. But in the average situation—say, the fiftyish widow—the balance of roles has not yet changed. The parent still considers herself the care-giver and protector. The children may be easily deceived by his or her intact outward appearance or, even more typically, feel embarrassed at disrupting that composure. For a while there is comfort for all in mutual bereavement, but after the space of a few months, both the widow and the children too often put a tourniquet on open grieving and resume the old order of emotional interaction. Worse yet, the mother may feel obligated to father or vice versa.

Over and over we hear widows say that while they may feel worse six or eight months later when no longer preoccupied with the flurry of paperwork and short-term coping, they hide those emotions from their children: "I don't want to worry them," "What can they do?" "They have their own lives to live." And, at the same time, children bury their latent grief because they don't want to make Mom cry. Then, also, as they become reinvolved with their "own lives," they are inclined toward quite a different set of criteria and program for what Mom should be doing with her life and how to tell her.

Keep the Lines Open

True, this thing called *communication* can be carried too far. Talking doesn't always solve the problem, but the widow's loneliness and the children's emotional conflicts are not lessened with silence either. Talking is almost always a better route. Children should know that appearances can be deceptive, yet not feel obligated to go along with a given scenario solely out of respect and politeness stemming from their past relationship with their parent.

A young woman seeking advice told me that she phoned her mother every Sunday morning from 2,000 miles away but felt even further distanced emotionally because her mother always said she was "as good as could be expected" in an even, cheerful voice. "How can I tell how she's really doing?" the daughter wanted to know. "She's my mother. I know she doesn't want to worry me." Well, for one thing: Don't call at the same hour, on the same day of every week, when mother is braced and ready for a particular verbal exchange. Phone at different hours, talk about what her day was like, ask about small happenings and avoid the inquisitional "What have you been doing?" and "Are you getting out?" But most important, confide your own feelings and remembrance and tell her what you are doing and—maybe—she will share hers. You are both on the threshold of a new, untried and possibly more equal relationship. Listen for the clues.

The way you handle your own grief will have a strong effect on your present relationship with your parent. In some families emotional containment is traditional and highly prized. Still unmentioned, 20 years later, is the time you, always the best, failed the big spelling test and the time you lost your one-day-old birthday wristwatch—all too mortifying to talk about. Growing up in a family like that has long-term effects. Can you share your grief and can you talk to your parent about his or her feelings, or do you bunch up inside and shut off any real communication because it's so uncomfortable?

Give Sympathy, Love, Understanding

You can alter the interaction even now by setting the example. Recently, while visiting in a small Idaho farming town, I saw a man cry 60 years of tears when his son embraced him and held him close for the first time in their adult lives, thus breaking the "manly" barrier his father had erected. The man's wife had died the year before, and he had not until then shed a tear—as he kept telling the friends who came to welcome the son, who had returned from an overseas tour of duty. Now he could cry.

However, even in families where communications are free and easy, mothers and offspring go through a period of readjustment. Even if you are fortunate to be the average child with the average parent, able to talk with one another and both adjusting to the loss as well as possible, you may still feel powerless and frustrated because you can't do more.

One thing is certain: You can't know the full extent of the lost relationship, nor can you become the surrogate husband or wife. There is a limit to your power. All your life you've known your parents as a pair: acting for, with and against each other. The surviving parent is now one person and neither he/she nor you know that person. Give sympathy, help, love and understanding, but not pity. If your eyes tell your mother you don't think she can make it, then she has two people to worry about—you and herself.

> *There is a limit to your power.*

Be In Touch, No Matter What

Nevertheless, just be aware that mothers who reject help, who, under the guise of independence, resolutely refuse "to burden" their already overly concerned children, may be a sham. Your mother may hesitate to let you know when she is sad and blue, reassure you that she is getting used to being alone and lull you into believing her. No matter how competent and controlled, all parents appreciate hearing from their children often and being reassured that they are loved and needed.

Mothers can be heard to mention three times in one sentence that all their children called last Sunday. It's easy for children to become caught up in their own lives and forget that it's been a long time since they wrote or phoned. No matter how independent she may seem, Mom likes to hear you invite her to visit, even if she lives next door. Don't be fooled by her protest that she understands how busy you are and knows she is always welcome.

Neither be fooled by her willingness to disrupt her life and become the kingpin in yours. On the surface it might seem to some that they are doing their mothers a favor when they turn childcare and other domestic tasks over to them. "Mom feels needed" is the rationalization offered by the children—as well as the avoidance excuse put forth by the widow herself. Such jobs are lonely jobs, however, and effectively close off the possibility for making a new life and new friends. Hardly ever is it a good idea to make mother the tail end of your own life.

> *No matter how independent she may seem, Mom likes to hear you invite her to visit, even if she lives next door.*

Whose Problem Is It?

Nor is it fair to present her with your financial problems at this stage in her life. If she has a little—or big—nest egg, she is going to be hard-pressed to turn you down for a loan or even keep from offering an outright gift. Mothers have a horror of becoming a financial burden on their children in later life and whatever funds she has now are important for that reason. Respect her need for independence—and also your own.

Going one step further, it is even less desirable to take over and take charge of her life. I suspect the in-charge son or daughter may be avoiding his or her own grief and anger by becoming busy and involved in details and numbers. Unless, of course, your parent is unable to manage and make decisions, a rule of thumb would be:

Don't take over and don't encourage helplessness by attending to whatever it is that needs attending to. At the time of death, everyone expects and makes room for bereavement and helping out, but children need to be sensitive to that which is appropriately within their province and that which is not.

Give Her Time

As discussed in earlier chapters, timetables vary in widowhood: The ability or inability early on to remove the personal belongings of the deceased, assume financial control and make necessary lifestyle changes is not the real indicator of a person's potential for adjusting. Two years later your mother can turn into a perfect butterfly.

For the children, time moves more quickly. They expect to see adjustment and changes in a year at the most, and that's another reason why mothers don't share their innermost fears and thinking with their children. When they feel miserable and weepy—especially after a period of relatively promising upbeat weeks—they don't dare reveal failure. Many a trip to a psychiatrist could be saved if the children would refrain from looking for cures or a panacea. Your mother has to rebuild her life on her own. You can certainly be part of the restructuring, but you cannot do it for her. Your energy will be better spent in teaching, encouraging, applauding and just being there rather than in "doing."

It takes more patience and time to encourage a parent who seems to have slipped into helplessness or never developed the necessary life skills than to assume control oneself. It's easier to write checks once a month than teach Mom how to keep her accounts; simpler to stop by the house for a 30-minute visit than get her involved in investigating outside interests. But if you teach her how to manage her accounts, make her own mistakes and survive them, she will be encouraged to try other difficult tasks.

If your tolerance is low, you lose patience easily and become exasperated with constant repetition, arrange for outside assistance for sharpening whatever skills mother is lacking. All sorts of mentors and agencies offer financial advice, tax assistance, nutrition classes and so on. Encourage her to join a widows' support group. When you are the only family member living close by, have the other siblings contribute to an "independence fund" to help mother gain self-confidence by acting for herself—anything from taxi fare to dancing lessons, to driving lessons, to adult-education classes.

One daughter I heard about enrolled her mother in an art class for a Christmas present; another took a gourmet-cooking class with her father, who hadn't known how to boil an egg up to then. The main idea is to encourage independence and to stand behind, not in front of, your parent. Applaud any accomplishment, no matter how small. Celebrate success and don't etch out a deeper groove of dependency by taking command.

As for the touchy, delicate little things like how she feels about celebrating certain anniversary dates, observing holidays, family visits and questions you wonder about, *ask,* and allow time for the discussion that follows and for the real truth to emerge. Never, never forget her birthday, though!

Once, in a widows' support group, one woman spoke longingly of the Navajo's custom of sending a grandchild to live with the widowed grandmother. Another woman quickly protested, "If I have a choice of ancient customs, give me suttee rather than a live-in grandchild." (Suttee, in case you don't know, is the old Hindu custom whereby the widow was cremated along with her husband.) So, you never know what will be right for any one person.

One last thought: You may see your parent as over the hill, and you may not be prepared for the very opposite of what we have been talking about. As parents move on from widowhood they may become people you never met before. She or he may be leading a very busy and active life, shedding years, wrinkles and heaven knows what else. Relax. Don't panic, and don't despair. You can try giving advice, but you'll probably be more effective if you take an objective view—you know, the way *they* did when you had one of those haircuts.

> *Never, never forget her birthday, though!*

Part 5

Resources

THE HELP THAT COMES FROM OUTSIDE OURSELVES is vital. Time alone is not curative—it takes people. Beyond the very early phases of widowhood, and once the help of family and friends has diminished somewhat, widows need to expand their support system and establish new social contacts. Mutual-help groups are the answer for many because they so neatly provide an opportunity for meeting people undergoing a similar life crisis and for forming relationships that may be extended beyond the group. "How To Start a Support Group," page 204, tells you more on the subject.

Also, I've included a section on "Books, Pamphlets and Organizations." Although you may not be able to concentrate on reading when you are first widowed, you will find dipping into books—however lightly—on the subject of grief and widowhood comforting. So peruse the library shelves and bookstores for books. Later, books on more specific topics of concern to you will be a wonderful source of information and inspiration. Some of these, as well as other resources, are included in the section.

How to Start a Support Group

CALLED *SUPPORT GROUPS, SELF-HELP GROUPS, MUTUAL-HELP GROUPS,* they all boil down to the same thing: a group of people sharing the same common problem and helping each other to cope with the problem; the end product is self-help.

It is like one great sigh of relief to find that others are going through the same thing and, of course, that is the very essence of mutual support. No one knows what it's like better than another widow—so hackneyed, yet so true. And even more frequently, you will hear the great majority of those who have participated say they found the support of other group members—usually strangers— more meaningful than help they received from doctors, clergy, lawyers or even family. As Phyllis Silverman, who pioneered the widow-to-widow concept, so neatly sums it up, "The learning offered does not come from a clinical sample or from a book, but from a fellow traveler's life experience."

Grieving time is compressed when widows and widowers are talking and listening to each other. Observing others model how to and how not to is a powerful way to process one's own grief. Mary dreads each new morning, Berta is doing aerobics, and Virginia is writing poetry. Helen, who was cheering Mary on last week, is lower than a bug this week. "But," she adds, "my bad times don't last as long; I've learned that much." Mary smiles her first smile in months. Agnes is ready to challenge Medicare to a duel, and several seconds have come forth to volunteer their services. Adeline is complaining about her neglectful children, and several of the others hear an echo of their own voice and grimace. "Come on, Adeline, get out of yourself," someone tells her. "If you want attention, stop whining; that'll shake them up!" The

Stay for two or three sessions at least.

ratio of laughing to crying is about 50-50. Someone talks about the terrible trials and tribulations of the past week and concludes by laughing at herself. Misery may like company, but try telling a joke to yourself. That takes a group.

It may not be for you. You'll have to step in and try it to find out. Stay for two or three sessions at least even if it checks out negatively; it may be more a matter of your own resistance than the group personality. Because a widowed-to-widowed group is such a good resource for making new friendships, you'll want to feel spiritually and philosophically in tune with some of the people, but don't put down diversity.

Finding a Widows' Support Group

To learn whether an established widows' support group already exists in your community, contact:

- ⊛ your local Information and Referral Service
- ⊛ Widowed Person's Service (WPS) of the American Association of Retired Persons (AARP). This organization maintains a very complete *Directory of Services for the Widowed in the United States and Canada.* It produces a quarterly newsletter for widowed women and men of all ages and will also provide material and leadership training for new groups.
  Write or call: AARP/WPS, 601 E Street NW, Washington, DC 20049; (202) 434-2260. Fax: (202) 434-6474.

If, after seeking and sampling, you find nothing right, start your own group. Organizing a small support group takes little more effort than finding three for bridge. In fact, start out with three other recent widows and have each one contact some others. You can obtain names from your doctor, church, synagogue, clubs and other likely referral sources—even personal ads and bulletin boards. If you're a young widow or a working mother, inquire at school, work or other places where you might find other, similar widows. Meet in one of the women's homes on a weekly basis for as long as you want. (A restaurant, or meeting for dinner, doesn't work out well because the

environment is inhibiting.) Set ground rules for:
- a regular meeting time,
- the time for beginning and ending the sessions, and
- respecting one another's personal confidences.

Keep the initial meeting leaderless. Begin by discussing books and articles on widowhood. It won't be long before individual topics and needs will emerge and take preference. And that's it. A support group fills a void in our crazy, complicated society. I think you'll find it worth the effort.

Extending Your Group's Reach

I should warn you, though, that you may get hooked. Before long you may want to make your group available to other widows, to widowers and still more widows. If so, here's how to proceed:

The best groups are free and open-ended so participants—limited, of course, to the widowed—may join without waiting or being restricted to discussing set topics. Leaders need not—and should not—be professionals, unless they themselves are also widowed. I have great respect for my colleagues in the field of counseling, but too often professionals have a strictly academic understanding of grief and their very presence may turn a self-help meeting into a therapy session. (Should you be looking for the professional touch, try a course on widowhood offered by local colleges or a private therapist. Some are very good.)

Now, to start a bona-fide widowed-to-widowed group, you'll need a committee of people interested in developing such a program. You can't do it alone. They may be all widowed people or include people drawn from the community, such as religious leaders, funeral directors, gerontology specialists, social-agency representatives, doctors and lawyers. Because the main job of the committee at this stage is to develop the framework for the organization, the group should be small and willing to work. Either as a member on the committee or as a participant willing to assist, recruit a social worker or psychologist to train peer counselors—later members of the support group may gain the confidence that comes with experience. Initially you'll want professional input. Once settled, recruit a lawyer for setting up the organization as a nonprofit corporation. Look for a generous businessperson who has office space available for your use and a media person to assist with publicity.

As for the location, avoid any facility that is not neutral; people are easily put off. Churches, synagogues and other religious institutions are *not* neutral meeting places. Members of one congregation do not necessarily care to attend another. Even within the same congregation there may be a built-in distaste for shifting from the role of patron to recipient. Don't locate in a mortuary; this may sound obvious, but people keep trying it. Cross off mental-health, public-welfare and senior-citizens' centers, as well as other social agencies that tend to classify people. Even a private home has a disadvantage; people seem to prefer a less personalized environment. Better to find a bank, library or public building that has space available for volunteer organizations and is accessible to the majority of people in the community.

A telephone is crucial. Don't change the number with great frequency (which is what happens when the phone is placed in the home of individuals). Get a permanent number. Use a telephone-answering machine if necessary, but arrange for a monitoring system to ensure that calls will be returned the same day. When no one is getting paid, you would be surprised how little funding is required. You'll need brochures announcing your services. By listing names of contributing firms—mortuaries, banks, insurance companies, trust lawyers, and the many others who have commercial contacts with widowed persons—the cost of printing is defrayed with money left over for other expenses. Grant money and government funding invite paperwork and require the kind of fiscal management that burdens new volunteer organizations. Support groups do not require large budgets; member contributions for postage and in-kind services from banks and merchants within your community ordinarily suffice.

Reach the widowed population by telling your story to the professional community (doctors, nurses, psychologists, hospitals, religious institutions and social agencies). Include the media (local newspapers and brochures that can be distributed to these sources;

radio and local TV stations, which provide public-service spots for good causes) and fraternal and business clubs.

Some support groups send out letters offering their services and personal visits to people whose names had been gathered from obituary notices and mortuaries. Other support groups are not comfortable with that approach and believe it to be intrusive. (Personally, I know if a visiting widow had contacted me shortly after my husband died, I would have considered her the ultimate Mrs. Busybody.) To join our support group, for example, people have to call us or just show up at the door. That's scary to many. Nevertheless, it's such an important first step that often just that act inspires new confidence. Both systems do work, however: For one, the effort is placed into developing individual trainees; for the other, the energy is channeled toward letting people know where you are.

Widowed-to-Widowed Group: Start-up Checklist

- ❏ Small committee to develop the program
- ❏ Professional input:
    - ❏ social worker or psychologist to train peer counselors
    - ❏ a lawyer, to set up group as a nonprofit organization
    - ❏ a media person to help get the word out
    - ❏ a generous businessperson, who could donate office space to the cause
- ❏ A neutral location for meetings
- ❏ A telephone with an answering machine
- ❏ Brochures announcing your services

Any support group tends to take on the personality of the leadership, and for that reason those who are taking responsibility for direction have to keep in mind the group's purpose and focus. Send prima donnas and needy egos elsewhere. Avoid cliques and divisive issues; keep discussions free of religion and politics. Continually groom new people for established jobs; a widowed-to-widowed group is a self-destructive organization in that people graduate when they leave. Board members might stay two or three years, but the strength of the organization is the willingness of its many different members to pass on to others what they have received.

Getting help is only half the magic of a support group; the other half—probably the better half—is giving help. When people accuse widowed persons active in support groups of working for their own benefit, they are absolutely right. I hope you'll find out for yourself.

It is like one great sigh of relief to find that others are going through the same thing and, of course, that is the very essence of mutual support.

Books, Pamphlets and Organizations

Grief and Widowhood

AARP/WPS. *On Being Alone.* 601 E Street NW, Washington, DC 20049. (Single copies free)

Caine, Lynn. *Being A Widow.* New York: Penguin, 1990.

Campbell, Scott & Silverman, Phyllis. *Widower.* New York: Prentice Hall, 1987.

Deits, Bob. *Life After Loss.* Tucson, Ariz.: Fisher Books, 1993.

Di Giulio. *Beyond Widowhood: From Bereavement to Emergence and Hope.* New York: Macmillan, 1989.

Gates, Philomene. *Suddenly Alone: A Women's Guide To Widowhood.* New York: Harper & Row, 1990.

Grollman, Earl. *Living When A Loved One Has Died.* Boston: Beacon, 1977.

Grollman, Earl. *Time Remembered: A Journal For Survivors.* Boston, Mass.: Beacon, 1987.

James, John W. & Cherry, Frank. *The Grief Recovery Handbook.* New York: Harper & Row, 1989.

Lukas, Christophera and Seidert, Henry M. *Silent Grief: Living in the Wake of Suicide.* New York: Charles Scribner's Sons, 1988.

Tatelbaum, Judy. *The Courage To Grieve*. New York: Lippencott and Crowell, 1984.

Tatelbaum, Judy. *You Don't Have to Suffer*. New York: Harper & Row, 1990.

For Children When a Parent Dies

Alderman Linda. *Why Did Daddy Die? Helping a Child Cope with the Loss of a Parent*. New York: Penguin Books, 1989.

Gaffney, Donna. *The Seasons of Grief: Helping Children Grow Through Loss*. New York: Penguin Books, 1988.

Grollman, Earl S. *Talking about Death: A Dialogue between Parent and Child*. Boston, Mass.: Beacon Press, 1990.

Marshall, Fiona. *Losing a Parent*. Tucson, Ariz.: Fisher Books, 1993.

LeShan, Edna. *Learning to Say Goodbye When A Parent Dies*. New York: MacMillan, 1976.

Career and Employment

Bolles, Richard, N. *What Color is Your Parachute? A Practical Guide for Job Hunters and Career Changers*. Berkeley, Calif.: Ten Speed Press, updated yearly.

Diaries and Journals

Baldwin, Christina. *One To One: Self-Understanding through Journal Writing*. New York: M. Evans, 1977.

Baldwin, Christina. *Life's Companion: Journal Writing as a Spiritual Quest*. New York: Bantam, 1990.

Jacobson, Gail B. *Write Grief—How To Transform Loss With Writing*. Menomonee Falls, Wis.: McCormick & Schilling, 1990.

Growth and Change

Butler, Pamela. *Self-Assertion for Women*. San Francisco, Calif.: Harper, 1992.

Butler, Robert N. & Lewis, Myrna I. *Love and Sex after Forty: A Guide for Men and Women for their Mid and Later Years*. New York: Harper & Row, 1986.

Friedan, Betty. *The Fountain of Age*. New York: Simon & Schuster, 1993.

James, John W. & Cherly, Frank. *The Grief Recovery Handbook: A Step By Step Program For Moving Beyond Loss*. New York: Harper & Row, 1988.

Neeld, Elizabeth Harper. *Seven Choices: Taking Steps to New Life after Losing Someone You Love*. New York: Delacorte Press, 1992.

Rubin, Lillian B. *Just Friends: The Role of Friendship in Our Lives*. New York: Harper Collins, 1986.

Russianoff, Penelope. *When Am I Going To Be Happy?* New York: Bantam, 1989.

Russianoff, Penelope. *Why Do I Think I'm Nothing Without a Man?* New York: Bantam, 1985.

Money Management

AARP, 601 E Street, NW, Washington, DC 20049 (Free)

D14168 *Final Details A Guide for Survivors When Death Occurs.*

D12380 *Money Matters.*

D11309 *Mastering Your Money.*

D13479 *Tomorrow's Choices: Preparing Now For Future Legal, Financial, and Health-Care Decisions.*

D13400 *Relocation Tax Guide: State Information for Relocation Decisions.*

Armstrong, Alexandra & Donohue, Mary. *On Your Own: A Widow's Passage to Emotional and Financial Well Being*. Dearborn, Mich.: Dearborn Financial Publishing, 1993.

Consumer Reports Editors. *Money Management Basics*. Yonkers, N.Y.: Consumer Reports, 1993.

Morris, Kenneth. *Wall Street Journal Guide To Money and Investment*. New York: Simon and Schuster, 1994.

Moving

Adams, Karen G. *A Complete Checklist and Guide for Relocation*. San Diego, Calif.: Silvercat Publications, 1994.

Nutrition and Cookery

Brody, Jane. *Good Food Gourmet,* New York: Bantam, 1992.

Brody, Jane. *Jane Brody's Nutrition Book*. New York: Bantam, 1982.

Castelli, William & Griffin, Glen. *Good Fat, Bad Fat: Lower your cholesterol and reduce your odds of a heart attack; revised* Tucson, Ariz.: Fisher Books, 1997.

Fisher, Helen. *Cookbook for the 90s*. Tucson, Ariz.: Fisher Books, 1989.

Shriver, Brenda & Tinsley, Ann. *No Red Meat*. Tucson, Ariz.: Fisher Books, 1989.

Support Groups

AARP/WPS. *Directory of Services for the Widowed in the United States*. 601 E Street NW, Washington, DC 20049. (202) 434-2260. Fax: (202) 434-6474.

Internet: aarpwrit@aarp.org

Silverman, Phyllis. *Widow-to-Widow*. New York: Springer, 1986.

Working with Volunteers

Morrison, Emily K. *Leadership Skills.* Tucson, Ariz.: Fisher Books, 1994.

Travel

Elderhosteling USA: *An Elderhostel How To Guide.* Ferndale, Calif.: Eldertime Publishing, 1991.

Hyman, Mildred. *Elderhostels: The Student's Choice.* Santa Fe, N.M.: John Muir Publications, 1991.

Palmer, Paige. *Senior Citizen's Guide to Budget Travel in Europe.* Babylon, N.Y.: Pilot Books, 1993.

Alcoholism

The National Council in Alcoholism, 733 Third Avenue, New York, N.Y. 10017.

Education Elderhostel, 100 Boylston Street, Suite 200, Boston, Mass. 02116.

Widowhood

FIAV: International Federation of Widows and Widowers, 10 rue Cambacérès, 75008 Paris, France.

National Association of Military Widows, 4023 25th Rd., N. Arlington, Va. 22207.

Parents without Partners, 8807 Colesville Rd., Silver Springs, Md. 20910.

Theos Foundation, The Penn Hills Mall Office Bldg., Pittsburgh, Pa. 15235.

AARP/WPS, 601 E Street, NW, Washington, DC 20049.

Part 6

The Widow's Survival Checklist

NOTHING IS SIMPLE ANYMORE. Death is followed by mounds of paper, stacks of forms that need to be filled out, countless decisions, and unsettling "firsts," all at a time when you are least able and willing to cope and attend to those demands. You can close your blinds to the outside world and to the challenge of living, as some widows and widowers do, or roll up your sleeves and get on with the job. For the latter, you have only one other choice: to do it the hard way or the easier way. Remember I said "easier," not "easy." From the depths of experience of widows before you, here are some suggestions for getting on with it:

For Paper, Facts and Money

One essential rule that applies to all transactions, and make no exceptions for the first six months, is to keep a copy of every letter you

Keep a copy of every letter you write related to the estate and a note of every phone call with the date, person you spoke to and outcome.

write related to the estate and a note of every phone call with the date, person you spoke to and outcome. Include sympathy calls, people who offer help and social engagements with time and dates. Maintaining this log will save you hours of hunting through scraps of paper and fruitless digging into the stubborn recesses of your mind. The chances are that you will forget more than you will remember and that you will search for more than you find.

- Request the funeral home to obtain 6 to 10 copies of the death certificate. Depending on the complexity of your estate, every claim will require an accompanying original certificate (as though you'd fake it!).

- Keep your numbers—your Social Security, his, bank accounts, medical insurance and so on—taped somewhere close to your desk for easy reference. Some days everyone wants a number.

- Notify Social Security, Veterans Administration, relevant business associates, employers, banks, fraternal organization and so on of the death.

- Change bank accounts to your name and establish a separate estate account for handling funds and bills.

- Hire a lawyer to take care of the will, probate, financial and property settlements. This is not always necessary when property is

If either lawyer or accountant is not performing to your satisfaction, change to someone else.

held with rights of 1 and no probate or taxes are required. When you hire an attorney, determine the fees and get an estimate of the total costs. Let him or her know at the outset that it is important to have the estate closed in the shortest possible time. Prolonged, dragged-out settlements are exceedingly wearing. Do the same with accountants; discuss fees and time schedules. Do not take a professional for granted because he or she is an old friend or was your husband's business acquaintance. If either lawyer or accountant is not performing to your satisfaction, change to someone else. I had three accountants before I found one who did not treat me as though I was an intelligent, but limited, chimpanzee.

- File insurance claims. Your agent can handle that for you. You may also have mortgage or credit insurance benefits, or some work-related policy of which you are unaware, so check that out too.

- Pay essential bills, such as mortgage payments and credit-and-

Do not pay any bills for which you have no knowledge or adequate information.

loan obligations that carry a penalty for late payment, but do not pay any bills for which you have no knowledge or adequate information. Consult your accountant. It is not unusual for unscrupulous people to submit unfounded claims. Also, hold off on medical bills until they are all in and you can have the extent of your liability and their accuracy verified. Hospitals pursue their claims quite aggressively; don't be swept away. If necessary, write to the doctors and hospital and tell them the cause for delay. Check all insurance possibilities with employers and governmental agencies.

• Transfer auto, real-estate titles and credit cards. If credit is in both names, you may find it simpler to make no change at this time. In many states credit may be easily established by the widow with a phone call to the credit bureau. Bond and stock titles can be changed directly or through a broker. Leave utility bill listings unchanged for the present, particularly if changing the listing means waiting on "hold" for an hour.

• Review auto, home and personal liability insurance with your agent to determine if changes are needed in coverage.

• Establish a simple bookkeeping system of "ins" and "outs," date and payer or payee. Then you don't have to agonize over small discrepancies in your checking account balance. Some widows make too much of a perfectly balanced, to the penny, checking-account. Banks don't give out test scores, although they do fault you for overdrawing. Introduce yourself to your local bank manager, request that they "cover your checks" from your savings and phone you in the event there is a problem. Also, stop by to say "hello" from time to time; bank managers change like the seasons. Deal with the bank that offers the best service.

Tackle what you can, forgive yourself your mistakes and never put yourself down.

Keep All Important Papers in a File

Begin collecting money-management information. Wait for a clear head and returned objectivity before making any decisions. Listen to everyone's advice and do nothing.

Take these tasks in the order of your particular circumstances and requirements. Some may not apply to you and in many cases there may be a far more complicated situation: a business that has to be managed, large debts and disputed wills, to name a few. Tackle what you can, forgive yourself your mistakes and never put yourself down.

For Your Peace of Mind

Keep a journal of your experiences and thoughts. Send notes or announcements to friends whom you wish to inform about the death. Some people prefer to use the telephone, some wait for Christmas and add a note to their card. But the longer you wait, the less likely you are to conclude the task and have it off your mind.

Allow the tears to flow and to feel sorry for yourself when you are feeling sorry for yourself. You need an audience for weeping. You can't cry alone, and you can't laugh alone.

Ask for help when you need it. Match the friends who sincerely offer their assistance and able family members with the jobs to be done. Many of the telephone calls, title changes, contacting and note writing can be assigned to someone or done more pleasantly with the company of a friend or family member.

> *Ask for help when you need it. Match the friends who sincerely offer their assistance and able family members with the jobs to be done.*

Plan your days, plan your weekends. Develop friendships with other single women and maintain the nurturing friendships and family ties that will tide you over the difficult times ahead. Don't go it alone. Let people know when you need them.

Inquire about a mutual-help group and attend at least three sessions.

For Home and Personal Security

Living alone takes getting used to. If, initially, you are apprehensive and afraid, don't think that will become your way of life. Without a man around the house, you will be more aware of sounds you never heard before and scary thoughts you never thought before. You will get better, but employ all sensible precautions to ease your mind and ensure your safety. Improve your home security to its maximum, but try not to become a victim of your own fears.

Installing a burglar-alarm system is expensive. However, if you can afford one that is connected to a central alarm, that's a good investment for the private home dweller. Apartment complexes that offer vigilant entry are likewise a good investment. In any case, you should have dead-bolt locks, bright outside lighting, variable automatic nighttime inside lights and all the additional precautions your police department will suggest upon inquiry—and you should inquire.

Never advertise that you live alone. Instead, throw out little comments to obscure that fact when dealing with repair men, sales people and such. If you're nervous about having someone come in for repairs, ask a neighbor or friend to come by. After a while you'll find trustworthy people you can use regularly.

When you go out alone in the evening stay in lighted areas for the coming and going. If you're driving, park under a street light, lock your car and have your key in hand ready when you return. Pockets are better than purses when possible. Be aware, but remember to enjoy yourself. Otherwise you might as well stay home with the dresser pushed against the door.

People use all sorts of ruses—cap guns, tapes of barking dogs, radios tuned to all-night talk shows—and keep on hand assorted weapons and devices. But obsession with crime prevention is not necessarily the best deterrent. Do what you can and then free your mind for better thoughts. Soon after I was widowed I was awakened by a burglar entering my house in the middle of the night and I reacted contrary to what I had ever imagined. I automatically called out, "Who's there?" Foolish question! I don't think I would have remembered tapes or caps. Fortunately, the intruder ran—with the television set. Later the police told me most burglars are there to steal, not murder. They prefer to make a hasty retreat if interrupted. Another widow told me, "If that ever happens again say, 'John, there's someone in the house, get the gun.'" I'm ready now, but also have an alarm system and am much more careful.

Many widows, especially those with health problems, feel better if someone calls daily to check up on them. In some communities such services are available through social agencies or private sources. If not, exchange morning calls with a friend or neighbor in a buddy system.

As for telephone listings, that is up to you. Some widows feel safer keeping their husband's name in the book because a female name or a single initial may elicit nuisance calls. My telephone business office claims a two-initial listing is less troublesome. I list my name but no street number as my solution and unplug the phone if necessary.

Make certain that you have working smoke-alarm units in your home and learn how to check them out.

Finally, read up on the many security hints provided by the police and in current magazine articles. Security is a problem all of us—not just widows—need to be concerned about.

For Your Health and Well-Being

Eat right, avoid excesses of alcohol, drugs, caffeine, sugar, tobacco. Nor is this the time for crash diets. Exercise and also find a relaxation routine such as yoga, massage, meditation, a walk in the park—a slant board—anything where you can free your mind from stress for some time during the day.

And last, in all matters and manner, be very, very nice to yourself. Listen to everyone's advice, but make no decision that is not based on your *own* opinion—no matter how long it takes to make one. Allow unsolicited advice to slip past you with a smile and a nod—and a deaf ear. Take your time; you will live again.

Index

Discipline of adolescent
children, 35
Disinterest, 77
Divorced women, 101-103
Doctors, anger toward, 26
Dreams, 49-53
Dumb remarks 11-15

E

Eating, 46-48
 breakfast alone, 21
 inappropriate, 46, 77
Elderhostel, 117, 210
Electrical repairs, 85
Emotional release, 9
Emotions, 19-20
Employment, 123, 150-155
 books about, 208
 and young widows, 184
Employment agencies, 151
Empty nest, 60
Entertaining couples, 143-144
Estate, 106-107
Exercise, 24, 77

F

Family
 changes in relationships, 88-96
 and sex, 119-122
Family counseling, 91
Finances, 123-132
 books about, 212-213
Funeral, 7-9

G

Grief and grieving, 1
 books dealing with, 210-211
 children's, 88-90
 duration of, 16-20
 and medication, 74

sex and, 184-185
and support group, 204
work and, 184
Growth, books about, 212
Guilt, 32-36
 anger internalized as, 27-28
 and dating, 113, 114, 116

H

Holidays, 97-100, 133-134
Homemaking, changes in,
 156-161
 repairs, 82-87
 security, 62, 220-222
 sharing, 160-161
House, keeping or selling, 127,
 156-159

I

Identity
 reestablishing, 146-149
 young widows and, 185-187
Indecision, 37-40, 104-112
In-laws, 92-93
 of young widows, 183-184
Insensitivity, 12
Insurance. *See* Life
 insurance
Investments, 124, 126, 129-132
 books about, 212-213
Invitations, 13

J

Job hunting, 150-155
 See also Employment
Jobs. *See* Employment
Journal writing, 64-68
 books about, 211
 examples of, 68-69, 135-137,
 175-176

106457